one
nation under
a groove

one nation under a groove

rap music and its roots

james haskins

JUMP AT THE SUN

HYPERION BOOKS
FOR CHILDREN
NEW YORK

To David Crouse

I am grateful to Kathy Benson and Ann Kalkhoff for their help.
A special thank-you to Ann Jordan.

Text copyright © 2000 by James Haskins

First Edition

3 5 7 9 10 8 6 4 2

Printed in the United States of America

Library of Congress Cataloging-in-Publication Data

Haskins, James, 1941–

One nation under a groove : rap music and its roots / by James Haskins. — 1st ed.

p. cm.

Includes bibliographical references and index.

Summary: Examines the origins and evolution of rap music, its African roots, and continuing popularity.

ISBN 0-7868-0478-5 (trade). — ISBN 0-7868-2414-X (lib.)

1. Rap (Music)—History and criticism Juvenile literature. [1. Rap (Music)—History
and criticism.] I. Title.

ML3531.H37 2000

782.421649—dc21   99-39765
                                          CIP

Visit www.hyperionteens.com

Photo credits can be found on p. 161.

This rhyme is mine and I lived to give it
So that the New Funky Nation can get with it
Understand the plan that's programmed
For all nations to slam the jam
One nation under a groove was the first move
 ——"New Funky Nation," Boo-yaa Tribe[1]

Contents

one nation under a groove

Now, even as we play
There's a new record sound goin' on today
We know your time is very precious so we won't stall
Just put some words together and tell ya all
That we're rockin' it (rockin' it y'all)
Rockin' it.
      —"Rockin' It," Fearless Four[1]

ON STREET CORNERS, IN PLAYGROUNDS,
throbbing from car stereos, and pulsing in time to
lurid lights in clubs, the music captures its listeners
with its beat, its excitement, its words. The music
thickens the air, filling it with sound and message,
mixing experience and emotion. This is rap: a music,
a lifestyle, a feeling, a speaking.

At first, rap music spoke about inner-city
African American culture. Today, though, rap music
has spread beyond the inner city and beyond the
United States to become a means of expressing a
worldwide experience. Rap has permeated all seg-
ments of society; the voice of rap now beats on the

door of the establishment with protest and emotion. Besides its formidable presence on CDs and the radio, rap is used in television ads, schools are filled with young people of all ethnic groups who have adopted hip-hop clothing styles, and movies utilize rap both as background music and as a means of conveying messages. For example, Warren Beatty's 1999 film *Bulworth* tells the story of a late middle-aged white senator who suddenly adopts rap (although somewhat awkwardly) to tell the truth and get through to his constituents. This diversification demonstrates the importance and influence of rap. As Lawrence A. Stanley observes, rap has become "the medium as well as the message."[2]

By definition, "Rap music is a combination of rhymed lyrics over rhythm tracks and pieces of recorded music and sounds called samples, taken from older records."[3]

Before the emergence of rap music, the term *rap* meant "to talk" and was often associated with con artists, or with attempts to be persuasive. With the advent of rap music around 1976, *rapping* came to mean talking, chanting, or singing in rhyme against a rhythmic background. Rhyming to the beat of music, until this time, had been called "emceeing." While many listeners are caught up in the sound, the beat, the storytelling, and the musical backgrounds against which the raps are set are also significant.

Rap lyrics are filled with social commentary, double meanings, hidden messages, allusion, and both anger and humor. The lyrics often evoke images of oppression and crime in American and other countries, criticizing in ways that call for black empowerment and the need for change. The lyrics are not always about oppression or crime, though. As Tricia Rose points out, "Frequently, the lyrics express the pleasures of black urban life," exulting that existence, and also playing with words, sounds, and images in a humorous manner.[4] Big Daddy Kane, for example, demonstrates the pleasure and power he finds in the rap experience itself in his rap "Smooth Operator" when he sings about "flowin'" to a slow tempo and about the "strength and power" found in rhyming and in rapping.[5] Big Daddy is "boasting," a tradition in rap music derived from reggae. He transmits to his listeners the pleasure he takes

Big Daddy Kane

in his lyrics and music, endowing both with a sense of fun.

Although many can understand the messages of rap lyrics and their origins, those not familiar with the urban black experience or black history may find the structure of the music of rap confusing. Whereas Western classical music is rooted in "its melodic and harmonic structures, the complexity of rap music . . . is in [its] rhythmic and percussive density and organization."[6] For rap music, the beat, articulated by percussion, is the dominant thing, rather than a melody, and this beat can take many forms, some seemingly inhospitable to ears accustomed to conventional commercial pop music. This emphasis on percussion, on the beat, has roots that extend back to Africa: "Dense configurations of independent, but closely related, rhythms, harmonic and nonharmonic percussive sounds, especially drum sounds, are critical priorities in many African . . . musical practices."[7]

Although it sounds spontaneous, the music of rap is usually formally planned out; only occasionally is it created at the time of the recording or performance by a DJ (as the creator of the music behind the lyrics is called, an abbreviation for "disc jockey") using the technical tricks of backspinning, scratching, and sampling. In many ways, the DJ must be both a skilled musician and an extremely knowledgeable technician with a sophisticated understanding of today's cutting-edge technology and an ear for what will fit best with the lyrics.

The techniques a DJ uses to create rap's background often require split-second decisions and a keen feel for what sounds best to back up the lyrics. These include: scratching (moving a record back and forth under the needle to create a beat), sampling (taking bits and pieces of previously recorded music and inserting them into the background of a rap, sometimes over and over again), and backspinning (moving a record back and forth by hand so that key phrases or beats are repeated over and over again). In addition, the DJ, in his sampling and backspinning, often creates allusions—references—to earlier musical styles and songs that interact with the lyrics, reminding listeners of the history behind the music and also offering new interpretations. The effect of all these techniques, when linked with percussion created by a synthesizer or drum machine, is to create a musical collage against which the rhymes are spoken.

The lyrics of rap songs are arranged in unique ways by each rapper. In rap poetry, words or syllables in a line are stressed because the *rapper* wants them to be stressed, not because ordinary pronunciation or some particular formula dictates that they be stressed. The stresses and rhymes in rap lyrics are frequently determined by the beat established by the singer or by the background music; the rhymes often are not regular and predictable. "Simply to recite or to read the lyrics to a rap song," Tricia Rose points out, "is not to understand them; they are . . . inflected with the syncopated rhythms and sampled sounds of the music."[8] The full meaning of rap lyrics frequently only emerges when they are sung and combined with the background music.

The *type* of rhyme in rap music, too, is varied. There is a great deal of internal rhyming, and half-rhymes are often used. These are rhymes in which only certain sounds of the rhyming words are identical, and the rest of each word may not rhyme in any way. Heavy D and the Boyz's "We Got Our Own Thang," for example, typically uses internal rhymes, half-rhymes, *and* full end-rhymes:

```
Everybody, shake your body, we don't ill, we
    chill at a party
Keep a groove that's sensual, three-dimen-
    sional, unquestionable
The lover is professional
Got a category, my own and I'm the president
Don't be alarmed, but I'm sewing up the
    resident
With my particular style, particular,
    extracurricular, smoother and trickier
Throwing on lyrics like you throw up a
    flapjack
You're a Chicken McNugget and I'm a Big Mac[9]
```

In this song, the "beat" of the lyric depends upon the separate rhythm established by the voice of the singer and by the accompanying tracks—the background music—rather than relying upon a beat that is inherent in the words of the "poem" itself. There are end-rhymes: "president" rhymes with "resident." Within lines, however, there are also internal rhymes, such as "ill" rhyming with "chill," and half-rhymes: the "al" sound in "sensu*al*" rhymes with the same sound in "three-dimension*al*," "unquestion*able*," and "profes-sion*al*." As most rap songs do, "We Got Our Own Thang" follows its own rules as it goes along; it does its "own thang."

Because rap does its own thing, it was initially surrounded by a great deal of controversy.
As Jimmy James notes in *The History of Rap*,
"Black, white, rock, and soul audiences continue to fiercely debate the musical and social
merits of rap, whose most radical innovation
subverted many of the musical and cultural
tenets upon which rock was built."[10] Many said
that rap wasn't "music" because it didn't have a
melody as most songs do. Others argued against
young people's listening to it because rap music,
and gangsta rap in particular, often uses obscenities, and the lyrics create verbal pictures of violence. The topics of many rap songs first made,
and still make, some people uncomfortable.
They deal with life surrounding the rapper, usually a black, urban milieu, and many of the
things that are commonplace to that life: alcohol,
drugs, sex, and violence. Rappers use their
music to criticize this way of life, often humorously, sometimes with anger, and to call implic-
itly or explicitly for change. Rap is sometimes
also used to express the pleasure the rapper
takes in his or her music and accomplishments;
then the song rocks with the rapper's boasting
and bragging.

Today, rap has firmly established itself as a part of American culture among black and white listeners alike, as well as among other groups. A 1999 article in *Time* pointed out that "Even if you're not into rap, hip-hop is all around you. It pulses from the films you watch . . . the books you read . . . the fashion you wear. Hip-hop got its start in black America, but now more than 70 percent of hip-hop albums are purchased by whites. In fact, a whole generation of kids—black, white, Latino, Asian—has grown up immersed in hip-hop."[11] Rap, which began as the voice of urban black youth, is now the voice of all youth: "Hip-hop . . . has compelled young people of all races to search for excitement, artistic fulfillment, and even a sense of identity by exploring the black underclass."[12] What the young people of the 1970s and '80s did was create a voice for their own culture.

In creating rap music, rappers are creating a sound that defines their generation. But in drawing on the past in their rhythms, sampling, and backspinning, as well as in their verbal references, they are also reminding themselves and their listeners of what came before them, of the history and the music of past generations of

African Americans. In many ways, rap is the voice of today's youth, but it is also the continuation of a voice that first spoke hundreds of years ago.

2

african rhythms

When you hear the tribal beat and the drums
[in rap music], they are the same drums of the
African past that draws the community to war. The
drumbeats are just faster, because the condition is
accelerating so they've got to beat faster.
— Sister Souljah[1]

tHE BEGINNINGS OF RAP MUSIC
are to be found hundreds of years ago and an
ocean away from the black urban neighborhoods
of the United States. In many West African
countries, music-making was the province of the
griots, male and female professional singers and
storytellers who performed using a variety of
techniques against a background of drums and
other musical instruments. Among the techniques used by a griot was call and response, in
which a solo verse line is alternated (answered)
by a choral response of a short phrase or word.

Griots were entertainers, keepers of history,
and commentators on the events of the present.

"A griot is required to sing on demand the history of a tribe or family for seven generations," Paul Oliver writes, "and, in particular areas, to be totally familiar with the songs of ritual necessary to summon spirits and gain the sympathy of ancestors. . . . He also must have the ability to extemporize on current events, chance incidents, and the passing scene. [Griots'] wit can be devastating and their knowledge of local history formidable."[2] The griot's position in society was that of keeper of records and more. Griots were highly esteemed, and as Wolfgang Bender observes,

A West Indian griot in the African tradition

The griots are rightly referred to as the archives and
libraries of this part of Africa. Thus the famous proverb,
"whenever a griot dies, a library dies." They were interpreters
of current politics, transmitting messages and orders from the
governing power to the people. As musicians with contacts with
other musicians outside the court, they were able to learn the
opinion of common people and could convey sentiments of the
populace to the ruler.[3]

In an oral culture, a culture without written records,
a griot held a place of great importance.

Although griots were the transmitters and
interpreters of current and past events, as are
many rap music artists today, individual tribal
members were also expected to have a good grasp
of their own spoken language. "This," K. Maurice
Jones points out, "was mandatory in order to gain
the respect on one's tribe and class. Mastery of
oral communication became, therefore . . . 'a prac-
ticed art, a challenge, a competitive sport, and a
hobby.'"[4] Just as rappers today are praised for
their verbal gymnastics, so, too, were griots
lauded, as well as those tribal members who could
display a quick verbal dexterity. To be able to
come up with a quick comeback or facile phrase
was a matter of pride among the members of the
various peoples of West Africa, a heritage that has
been passed down to the present.

During the time slave trading was rife, these oral traditions traveled with the slaves from Africa to the New World. Many of these slaves came from West Africa, home of the griot tradition, and although slave traders and owners attempted to destroy the traditions of those they had enslaved, slaves not only retained many of their oral traditions but added to them despite the horrific conditions of their enslavement. Forbidden by their owners to learn to read and write—although many did learn in secret—the griots kept alive the slaves' history and traditions and served other purposes as well. "Letters and diaries exist in which eighteenth- and nineteenth-century American and European travelers in the American south recorded their impressions of the 'wild and primitive' music of black slaves," Ralph Eastman writes. "Some writers mentioned the strong emotive power of the dissonant singing. All, however, dismissed the music as a curious and bizarrely spontaneous expression of a primitive people."[5] Had these travelers known the significance of many of the songs and their music, they might not have been so dismissive.

Although many of the songs and their accompanying music were "hollers" or "work songs"—

sounds and songs to coordinate the work of groups of people—others had intricate double meanings, as K. Maurice Jones points out:

> A lyric like "I ain't got long to stay here," from the spiritual "Deep River," superficially meant that a slave was about to die and looked forward to life in the Promised Land, or Jordan. However, for many slaves, the song often signaled the local presence of Underground Railroad conductors like Harriet Tubman, who risked their lives to help courageous slaves escape the misery of bondage.[6]

Some songs alerted the slave population to the opportunity to escape; others gave directions on ways to go in that escape, as in the spiritual "Wade in the Water":

```
Wade in the water,
Wade in the water, children,
Wade in the water,
God's gonna trouble the water.
'Member one thing an' it's certainly sho',
Wade in the water,
Judgment's comin' an' I don' know,
Wade in the water.[7]
```

In this song, sinners are seemingly urged to follow a righteous path through life. On another level, the song also gives instruction on escape techniques. Trackers with their dogs could not follow the scent of an escaping slave if he or she took to water, wading in a stream or river.

Just as many of the songs—like those of the earlier griots—evolved out of the conditions faced by the enslaved Africans, so did the accompanying music. The rhythmic emphasis of African music was transplanted and added to the melodic music of the New World, resulting in work songs and spirituals that had a strong melody as well as a strong, definitive beat. There also evolved songs that utilized the call-and-response technique heard in the griot's performance in which the singer sings a phrase and the audience responds either in song or by commenting on the singer's performance or message.

When the African slaves reached the Americas, they were usually forced to convert to Christianity, the religion of their masters. The religious services they developed reflected many of the traditions the slaves had carried with them across the seas. For example, in Haiti, which was controlled by the French, slaves were forced to convert to Catholicism. Haitian slaves easily combined the Latin Mass and Catholic beliefs with their own religious traditions, creating what is now known as *vodun*, or *voodoo*. Catholic

saints conveniently fit into the pantheon of *loa*,
powerful spiritual figures of African tradition,
and voodoo ceremonies combined and continue
to combine rituals from African beliefs with the
traditional Latin Mass. In Jamaica, where first
Catholicism was forced upon the slaves by the
Spanish, and then Protestantism by the British,
religious services were often enlivened by both
the call and response of the griots and the distinctive beat of *burru* drumming, virtuoso African
drumming on *akete* drums.

In the United States, most Southern slaves
were forced to adopt Protestant beliefs, but again,
they shaped these beliefs in unique ways:

> The services of the slaves were reminiscent of religious
> ceremonies in Africa. They were lively, uplifting affairs com-
> plete with music, chanting, and spiritual possessions. . . . The
> high point of the service was the preacher's sermon, or call,
> and the congregation's response. . . . Ministers expected the
> congregation to interrupt their sermons with applause and affir-
> mations of "Tell it like it is!" . . . Centuries later . . . rap and
> hip-hop . . . would continue the tradition of call and response
> that began in slave churches with a crew encouraging a rapper
> . . . with "Go 'head!" or "Word!"[8]

As in the spirituals the slaves sang, several
things were happening at once at such services.

What appeared on the surface to be a lively rendering of the usually staid Protestant service by a group of slaves was, in fact, a continuation of the traditions from their homeland, with, as Jones points out, the preacher serving in the role of griot.

In similar ways, musical instruments of European design were adapted to the strong, rhythmic music of the slave. When captured in Africa, slaves were forced to leave all their possessions behind. They were loaded like cattle onto slave ships with nothing more than the clothing they were wearing, and often even that was taken from them. The drums and stringed instruments that had enlivened and enriched their lives were left behind. In America, "Musicians either had to build their own instruments or, more commonly, adapt existing European instruments for their purposes. Essentially, these folk musicians approached the playing of European instruments with an African consciousness, thereby synthesizing a new form of music."[9] In the early nineteenth century, this music and the dances accompanying it inspired, among other things, minstrel shows which came to be usually performed, ironically, by white performers:

The vigorous, syncopated songs and dances of the Negro
slaves so impressed white troubadours in the early 1800s that
they attempted to interpret them in blackface acts in stage
shows and circuses. Unfortunately, a blackface tradition of
another sort had already been established in both America and
England—a tradition rooted much less in appreciation of the
Negro's music than in crude parodies of his dialect and rigid
stereotyping of his behavior and appearance. Music and carica-
ture were inevitably interwoven, and the result was the minstrel show.[10]

An 18th-century Caribbean festival

Minstrel-show performers in blackface made use of the musical instruments employed by the slave population: banjos, tambourines, and bone castanets. These were originally made by the slaves from materials at hand when they were forced to entertain their white owners.

The most popular form of music from 1896 until 1917, ragtime, originated in the minstrel shows, the name meaning "ragged time . . . [which refers to] the music's syncopated, off-beat rhythm."[11] Through their performances, although they were degrading to blacks, the blackface performers spread an awareness of "Negro melodies" to Americans in the North who, until that time, had no knowledge that such music existed.

Although ragtime music found great popularity with white audiences, it was not until after the Civil War that the white population became aware of the full range of African American music. In the 1860s, attempts were made to transcribe black spirituals and work songs and bring them to the public's attention, but only after 1865 were blacks permitted to perform their own music publicly, and then usually only for black audiences.

After the Civil War, black men and women, although free, had few options or opportunities. Many continued working for nominal pay on the same plantations where they had labored as slaves. Some left the plantations, but the jobs open to them were menial and low paying. Others turned to music to earn a living, performing in minstrel shows they themselves organized, performing as individual musicians, or singing in choirs.

For example, George L. White, a former Union soldier teaching at Fisk University in Nashville, Tennessee, organized a choir made up of black students after the Civil War. In 1871, White arranged a concert tour for the choir to raise money for the school. The choir, which usually sang classical selections, was highly unsuccessful with white audiences until they gave up the classical songs and sang some of the spirituals that were part of their culture. The choir quickly gained fame and popularity as the Fisk Jubilee Singers, and even performed in Europe to acclaim. Their performances were equally lauded in the United States. One white audience member in Brooklyn wrote to the New York *Tribune* praising the Jubilee Singers:

Allow me to bespeak a universal welcome through the
North for these living representatives of the only true native
school of American music. We have long enough had its coarse
caricatures in corked faces; our people can now listen to the
genuine *soul-music* of the slave cabins.[12]

The performance of African American music,
however, was not confined to minstrel shows and
black choirs only, nor was the music itself static.
Individual musicians utilized elements of the
"hollers," work songs, spirituals, and the call and
response of the black churches, and experimented
with rhythm and sound. From this experimenta-
tion, a new music emerged among black musicians: the blues.

The blues had humble beginnings, but it
quickly became popular beyond its roots.
Folklorist Alan Lomax points out that in the late
nineteenth century, "the blues lived in the wild
and melancholy cries of the mule-skinners and
roustabouts of the Mississippi. . . . The earliest
blues consisted of lines from work songs and
hollers repeated four times to a steady beat on a
guitar."[13] Because this music grew out of the
nineteenth-century rural black experience, it is
now referred to as "country blues." The songs
were usually performed by itinerant singers who

traveled from one black community to another, much like the griots of Africa, singing for pennies and spreading their music. Later, these songs and hollers and their style were adapted by professional musicians in their compositions, becoming popular in both black and white urban communities.

As with spirituals and work songs, the blues were no one person's property; songs that became popular would be learned and reinterpreted by each musician, who would usually add to them with his own improvised lyrics and instrumental arrangement. Often individual singers would attempt to outdo one another in their interpretations, just as "many years later, rappers would also repeat the tradition of competition by rapping over the same backing tracks and samples."[14]

Although improvisation initially dominated both the lyrics and the music, the structure of the blues became more formalized around the turn of the century. What we think of now as the blues is expected to follow an eight-, twelve-, or sixteen-bar (or measure) formula, have an aab rhyming structure, and use the "blue notes," the minor seventh, diminished fifth, and minor third. "The most distinctive melodic characteristic of the blues is the use of microtones (intervals smaller than a half step), commonly called bent pitches . . . used most often on the third and seventh notes of the scale."[15]

By the 1920s, blues had become popular enough with black audiences that the fledgling record companies of the time felt it was worth it to record some of the singers:

The first and finest of Negro folk blues composers to make commercial recordings was Blind Lemon Jefferson, who had earned his living for many years playing in the joints up and down the Frisco railroad track in Dallas, Texas. . . . His records sold so fast that the Paramount Record Company gave them a special label, trimmed in lemon.[16]

The success of these "race records," as records made expressly for black audiences were then called, brought other blues musicians to the attention of the recording industry, which realized the money to be made with such music. Quickly following Blind Lemon Jefferson into the recording studio were Mamie Smith, Leadbelly, Bessie Smith, Jelly Roll Morton, Charlie Patton, Robert Johnson, and W. C. Handy, who is called "the father of the blues." African American entrepreneurs also took

an interest in these blues artists, and in 1921, Dr.
Harry Pace founded Black Swan records. Although
the company was bought out in 1924, it distin-
guished itself both by being the first black-owned
record company, and by the quality of talent it
attracted. Blues had a wide audience, and realizing
this, during the late 1920s, Columbia Records and
other companies who predominantly recorded
white artists began sending mobile recording studios to various Southern states to record a variety
of country blues musicians.

Although blues is thought to express the
painful essence of the black experience, the
opposite is often true. "While the blues may feature harsh and 'mournful' sounding performances
of downbeat lyrics," Ralph Eastman notes, "its
totality is nonetheless a raucous, crude, ironic and
rhythmic dance music. . . . The blues is the catalyst
that brings temporary relief from a life of
drudgery, not a catalog of those drudgeries."[17]
Blues lyrics complain, criticize, insult, and often
humorously comment on people as well as conditions—especially those of a sexual nature. In this
respect, the blues shares a great deal with rap
music; both seek to comment, to entertain, and to
voice a desire for change.

Just as the spirituals, work songs, and hollers led to the development of the blues, so, too, did the blues evolve. During the 1920s, in the cities of the North and South, in Kansas City, Chicago, and New York, a new sound was being heard that had originated in the late nineteenth century in New Orleans—Dixieland jazz:

> In its beginnings, jazz was more an approach to performance than a body of musical compositions. The black marching bands of New Orleans, which often accompanied funeral processions, played traditional slow hymns on the way to the cemetery; for the procession back to town, they broke into jazzed-up versions of the same hymns, ragtime tunes, or syncopated renditions of popular marches.[18]

The instruments used in jazz were those used in a band—trumpet, cornet, clarinet, and trombone—added to which were drums or a string bass to provide a heavy rhythm.

During the early decades of the twentieth century, more and more blacks were moving northward to seek work and greater opportunities than the Jim Crow South could offer. Along with them, they carried their music, and by the 1920s, the Jazz Age was in full swing. In 1923, jazz recordings for black audiences were made by King Oliver's Creole Jazz Band, which at that

Louis Armstrong

time included trumpeter Louis Armstrong. The
recordings that reached middle-class white
America, however, were often made by white jazz
musicians. Just as, earlier, minstrel shows had
appropriated black song and dance, and white
musicians had adopted both country and city
blues' styles, white musical groups quickly followed
in the footsteps of black groups, imitating the
black jazz styles.

Like blues, jazz combines both Western and
African influences. It is "characterized by improvisation, the spontaneous creation of variations on
a melodic line, by syncopation, where rhythmic
stress is placed on the normally weak beats of the

musical measure, and by a type of intonation that would be considered out of tune in Western music."[19] Again, the traditional call-and-response technique is frequently employed both instrumentally—one instrument echoing or answering a first, the second instrument trying to outdo the first in creative improvisation—and in its lyrics (sung and spoken). Cab Calloway, for instance, would mix his trademark phrase, "Hi-dee-hi-dee-ho," which was enthusiastically repeated by audiences, with call-and-response scatting, as in his 1933 song, "Zah-zuh-zah."

Jazz was wild, crazy, cool, hep, jive; it had its own language and lifestyle, and like rap music today, often unsettled the older generations. Many songs contained references to drugs and sexual behavior that scandalized parents of the younger generation, which loved the new sounds. One response was a series of "cabaret laws" passed in New York City in the 1920s. These, according to Tricia Rose, "restricted the places where jazz could be played and how it could be played. These laws were attached to moral anxieties regarding black cultural effects and were in part intended to protect white patrons from jazz's 'immoral influences.'"[20] The laws delineated what kind of jazz could be played, on what type of instruments, and who could play it—restrictions that were a direct antithesis to the freewheeling music itself.

Jazz would persist and survive, however, and when rap music was introduced in the last third of the twentieth century, some rap artists would hark back to their jazz roots in their own compositions. Rap artist Guru, in his *Jazzmatazz, Volume 1*, for example, uses jazz extensively and evocatively. In 1993, Guru stated that he uses jazz because "I want to make older people appreciate hip-hop and get my homeboys to appreciate jazz. It's a family-type thing."[21]

In the 1930s, although "hep" jazz continued to be played, the music was again evolving. Swing became popular during this time, with big bands playing highly arranged, orchestrated versions of jazz that were easier to dance to than the jazz created by smaller groups. Both black and white big bands became known for a smooth sound that appealed to older generations. In opposition to the rigidity and size of the big bands and appealing more to the younger generation, "bop," or "bebop," emerged in the 1940s, led by Charlie Parker, Dizzy Gillespie,

Thelonious Monk, and others.[22] Bebop meant a return to small bands and to the individual improvisational solo. Its erratic rhythms, however, and the variety of its improvisation made it difficult to dance to.

Blues musicians, too, were moving on. During the 1930s, older country blues artists were finding that "although the newly urbanized African American audiences still loved their music, acoustic instrumentation was not sufficiently loud either to overcome or reflect the din of modern city life. . . . Enterprising musicians switched to electric guitars, added drums, and further amplified their sound."[23] In the cities of both the North and South, blues was being transformed, changing yet again. The path led to the development of the "Chicago Blues," urban blues, or city blues style by such musicians as, initially, Big Bill Broonzy, Memphis Minnie,

Charlie Parker

and Tampa Red, and, later in the 1950s, Muddy
Waters and Howlin' Wolf. City blues followed
the structure of the traditional blues, but utilized
the new musical technology of the day.

Within the recording industry, the music produced by these city blues players, by black big
bands, and by bebop musicians—the black music
of the 1940s—came to be lumped together under
the term *rhythm and blues* (R & B), a phrase that
came to be an industry replacement for the term
race records. The term quickly expanded to
include small bands and black teenage harmony
groups, and came to be a general term covering a
wide variety of music that combined elements of
city blues, spirituals, and jazz. Black musicians
such as Elmore James and Chuck Berry were
also experimenting with rhythm and blues,
increasing the beat to double time, creating a
type of R & B that later would come to be known
as "rock 'n' roll."

Hundreds of records were sold, and the music
of the day was played constantly on the radio by
black disc jockeys who added their own flair to
the mix. In the 1940s and '50s, the DJs, just as
rappers do today, introduced the records with
rhymes and hep slang. Dr. Hep Cat (Lavada

Durst), a black radio DJ in Austin, Texas, for example, was known for his jive couplets:

```
If you want to hip to the tip and bop
    to the top
You get some mad threads that just
    won't stop.24
```

It was the era of the hep cat and the zoot suit, and black radio stations across the country swayed not only with the music, but with the rhythm of the raps that DJs were using to introduce the music.

All this innovation in black music did not go unnoticed in the white segment of American society. The music being produced was exciting and innovative, and much of it was great to dance to. Recognizing its possibilities, white musicians were soon imitating and borrowing from black musicians who had created a sound that electrified young audiences. In 1951, that style of music was given a name when disc jockey Alan Freed referred to it on his radio show as "rock 'n' roll."

More and more white artists were borrowing from African American rhythm and blues artists. The record industry, "observing the success of rhythm and blues and rock 'n' roll songs distributed on 'race records' . . . issued covers—competing 'sanitized' versions of the same songs, but recorded by white artists."[25] Although later black artists such as Chuck Berry and Fats Domino would cross over and gain popularity with both black and white audiences, many of the early rock 'n' roll hits by white artists of the 1950s were originally rhythm and blues hits that had first been recorded by black artists. The most well known of these white artists was Elvis Presley. With his popularity, rock 'n' roll was here to stay.

Time to talk about a hardcore buff
Who played rock and jazz and even classical stuff
He rocked it and jazzed it and treated it nasty
Until it all sounded like the theme from "Taxi"
— Sub Sonic 2, "Unsung Heroes of Hip-hop"[1]

IN 1954, THE UNITED STATES SUPREME
Court ruled in the case of *Brown* v. *The Board of Education of Topeka, Kansas* against the inequality of segregated schooling. The impact of this one ruling on American society during the next two decades was phenomenal. Suddenly, the highest court in the land was saying what African Americans had known for hundreds of years: they had been and were being viewed and treated as second-class citizens. Black leaders arose to lead the struggle for equal rights: Rosa Parks, Martin Luther King, Jr., Malcolm X, Jesse Jackson, and many others. Like any major upheaval, the struggle was not without violence or victims, but by the

1970s, major legislation on the federal level had desegregated the nation's schools and social change was irreversible.

The civil rights movement of the 1950s and 1960s, while beginning to right some of the wrongs that had persisted for centuries, also opened up the predominantly white music industry to black artists of every type. Gone were "race records" and "rhythm and blues" records; black artists were recording with major record companies, and their records were being marketed to both black and white audiences. Doo-wop, a funkier rhythm and blues, was popular on inner-city streets. One of its big commercial hits, "This Chick's Too Young to Fry," recorded by a "gangsta" doo-wop group, the Prisonaires, foreshadowed gangsta rap. Bobby Robinson of Enjoy Records recalls,

> Doo-wop originally started out as the black teenage expression of the '50s and rap emerged as the black teenage ghetto expression of the '70s. Same identical thing that started it—the doo-wop groups down the street, in hallways, alleys, and on the corner. They'd gather anywhere and, you know, doo wop doo wah da da da da. You'd hear it everywhere.[2]

In the midst of this music revolution, however, one record company suddenly emerged head and shoulders above others in promoting black artists: Motown Records of Detroit, Michigan.

In 1957, a young musician named Smokey Robinson was lead singer for a group named the Matadors. During an unsuccessful audition, the group was heard by a young black man named Berry Gordy, Jr. He recognized the group's talent and persuaded them to work with him, changing their name to the Miracles. Robinson, in turn, urged Gordy to start a record company, and in 1959, after borrowing $800 from his family, Gordy created Motown Records in inner-city Detroit. As Sharon Davis points out in *Motown, the History*, "It is probably true to say that Motown was as much Robinson's company as it was Gordy's, although Gordy was unquestionably the head of the company."[3]

The "Motown sound" included girl groups such as the Supremes and the rhythm and blues of Smokey Robinson, but came to be mainly identified with the sound of "soul music," a blend of gospel and rhythm and blues that had emerged in the late 1940s and early 1950s. "The two most important names in 1950s soul music . . . were James Brown, whose [first record in] 1956, 'Please, Please, Please,' had all the raw urgency of

black preaching, and Ray Charles, whose 1959
'What'd I say?' took the sound to a wide audience."[4] Motown's soul sound proved extremely
popular. Soul music caught on with audiences of
every race, and by 1966, three out of every four
Motown releases were hitting the top ten on the
record charts.[5] During the 1960s and '70s,
Motown was *the* record company for black artists,
including Gladys Knight and the Pips, Stevie
Wonder, Marvin Gaye, and the Temptations. The
Motown artist who was to have the greatest impact
on later rap music, though, was James Brown.

James Brown was born on May 3, 1933, in
Augusta, Georgia, and grew up just as blues, jazz,

James Brown

and bebop were hitting their peaks of popularity.
Combining rhythm and blues, gospel, and the
keen sense of drama characteristic of the black
pulpit, Brown's performances were sellouts, as
were his records, the style of which was widely
imitated. The early songs of soul artists followed
the trends of rock 'n' roll, singing of love or, like
Chubby Checker, of dances such as the Twist. As
the music evolved, however, under the leadership
of Brown in particular, it began to deal with the
black experience and with black pride. "By 1967,
Brown had traded his straightened hair for an
Afro, or 'natural' hairstyle . . . [and his song lyrics]
began to reflect the self-determination and pride
that was sweeping America."[6] In his "Say It Loud
(I'm Black and I'm Proud)," for example, Brown
raps about African Americans pushing ahead and
never quitting until "we get what we deserve."[7]
"Say it Loud," as well as Brown's "Funky
Drummer" would later become the most-sampled
tracks in rap music, not only for their messages of
empowerment, but for their pounding beat.

Brown's lyrics and raps were reinforced by a
heavy percussion with a driving backbeat and
rhythm, elements that have frequently been
"sampled" from his records and used to back up

the raps of artists of the late 1970s, '80s, and '90s. Brown has been called the "Godfather of Soul," but in many ways, he is also the Godfather of Rap. Like earlier artists, and later, rappers, he often rapped during his songs in addition to singing, and his music had an electrifying rhythmic presence that entranced audiences, spoke to them, and kept them dancing.

During the 1970s, the complex beat of Brown's music was picked up by other musicians and used in ways he never anticipated. Disco music became the rage in America, combining the heavy rock beat seen in Brown's compositions—sometimes mixed with the sounds of Latin percussion instruments—but using a fast jazz tempo. Disco was more than a kind of music, however; as with the blues and jazz, it was a lifestyle. The 1977 movie *Saturday Night Fever* spread disco beyond the nightclubs of the big cities and into the small towns of America. Suddenly, nightclubs, town dances, even high-school proms were lit by the flashing, round disco ball and strobe lights hallmarked by the film, and dancers were imitating actor John Travolta in their dramatic disco dance moves.

One reason for disco's popularity was that it

required a partner, unlike earlier dances such as the Twist that could, in a pinch, be danced solo. But the formality of the dance style and the music also drew negative comments. As Maurice K. Jones says, "Popularized by groups like the Village People and the Bee Gees, disco sounded as if it were constructed by robots or computers, not created by human beings."[8] What was important in disco was its beat and how easy it was to dance to; individual innovation and creativity were not important ingredients in creating this type of music.

Although introduced in the black and gay clubs in New York, disco music quickly became synonymous with "white" music, and many young African Americans rejected it both because of its lack of opportunities for individual musical expression, and its lack of significance to the black experience. In the black neighborhoods of the cities, other ways of self-expression were beginning to catch on that spoke more directly to these young people. Although the heavy beat of disco was appealing, the set moves of disco dancing were not. So, again, as with earlier forms of African American music, these young people were improvising, adapting, and making a music of their own.

• • •

On the island nation of Jamaica, a new kind of
music was becoming popular at the same time
disco was sweeping the United States. Since the
early 1940s, dances, called "blues dances," had
been held in Jamaica's black ghettos. They were
held in large halls or out in the open, and the most
popular music played during the 1950s was
American rhythm and blues, which had been
introduced to the island by American sailors sta-
tioned there.[9] The music was provided by records
played by a DJ and huge "sound systems." A
sound system was not merely a turntable and
speakers; when Jamaicans referred to a sound
system, they meant the equipment plus the DJ,
roadies, engineers, and bouncers needed to control the crowds. Sound systems were large mobile
discotheques that went from place to place to
provide music for dances.

As sound systems developed, the crowds
drawn to them demanded only the newest, coolest
music. In response to this, not only did system
owners travel to the United States to obtain the
latest records, but a burgeoning record industry
developed in Jamaica itself, creating music that
incorporated American rhythm and blues, but

added a distinctive island flavor to it. Among the
musical styles created between 1961 and 1967
was ska, which was heavily based on a combination of American rhythm and blues, jazz, and doo-
wop, but with a wilder, more jerky beat. Then, in
1968, came reggae, the music that has become
intimately associated with Jamaica and
Rastafarianism. In reggae,

> The beat was distinctive . . . in that it dropped any of the
> pretensions to the smooth, soulful sound that characterized
> slick American R & B, and instead was closer . . . to U.S.
> southern funk, being heavily dependent on the rhythm section
> to drive it along.[10]

Reggae incorporated Jamaican sound with
social protest and the expression of Rastafarian
beliefs. Although Jamaican immigrants to
America brought this music with them, the 1973
film *The Harder They Come*, starring reggae
singer Jimmy Cliff, is generally credited with
spreading reggae's popularity throughout the
United States. That same year, a Jamaican group
called The Incredible Bongo Band recorded its
cover version of "Apache," a track that, like those
of James Brown's, has been heavily sampled by
rap musicians.

As the DJ dances in Jamaica became more popular, individual DJs (or "selectors") became recognized for their artistry with their sound system and for their skill in "toasting," talking over the records to encourage people to respond vocally or to dance to the music. This tradition of talking in rhyme over music was well established in the Caribbean islands. Dub poets in Jamaica recited their poetry against a background of drums and reggae instrumentation, using the voice also as an instrument. In Trinidad during the 1970s, a type of elaborate calypso with talking, called rapso, had also emerged. Chako Habekost, of *The Beat* magazine, writes that, "rapso developed . . . around the same time as dub poetry. Fueled by the period of social unrest and political activism, rapso became the mouthpiece of the underprivileged masses of Trinidad and Tobago."[11]

Following in the footsteps of the dub poets, the rapso artists, and the reggae singers of their own island, Jamaican DJs rhymed to music, but without the element of protest. They assumed colorful, easily identifiable names, such as Count Machuki (one of the first talking DJs). Sound system owners also had memorable names— Duke Reid, Sir Coxsone, Prince Buster, and "King" Edwards—

that became legendary among their listeners. Each system had its own loyal fans, and "battles" were common among different DJs and their sound systems. The various sound systems would travel around the island, playing and competing with other systems and their DJs.

These "battles," or competitions between DJs and their sound systems became the rage, with each trying to outdo the other in music, toasting, and verbal quips. Part of the skill in operating the sound system was the engineer's facility in "dubbing," cutting back and forth between the vocal and instrumental tracks while adjusting the bass and treble for maximum effect.[12] This emphasized the beat and allowed the DJ an opportunity to rhyme and toast. All this was paving the way for the techniques used in rap music. As Henry A. Rhodes points out, rap and reggae shared a great many similarities:

First, both types of music relied on pre-recorded sounds. Second, both types of music relied on a strong beat by which they either rapped or toasted. American rap music relied on the strong beat of hard funk and Jamaican "toasting" relied on the beat from the Jamaican rhythms. Third, in both styles the rapper or toaster spoke their lines in time with the rhythm taken from the records. Fourth, the content of the raps and toasts were similar in nature. . . . There were boast raps, insult raps, news raps, message raps, nonsense raps, and party raps.[13]

DJing and toasting came to the United States in the 1970s, but one man is credited with its mutation into rap. Clive Campbell, also known as Kool Herc, is often said to have been the first modern rapper. Campbell was born in Jamaica and moved with his family to the Bronx borough of New York City. He had gotten his nickname, Hercules, for his physical build, but he didn't like that name so he shortened it to "Herc," adding "Kool" when he became a graffiti artist. Around 1973, Campbell put together a sound system like those in Jamaica, and in 1975, began to play various clubs and dances. During his performances, he threw in simple rhymes and comments as did the DJs in Jamaica, but he became most famous for his skill with his system:

> Kool Herc seldom played an entire song. He knew which part of the record sent his audience into a frenzy. It was usually a 30 second "break" section in which the drums, bass, and rhythm guitar stripped the beat to its barest essence. Herc used two turntables to accomplish this feat. This technique became known as "beats" or "break-beats."[14]

With these "breaks," a style of dancing emerged to take advantage of the strong beat, one that showcased the dancer's acrobatic skills: break dancing.

Break dancing was a significant part of the entire hip-hop culture that emerged in the Bronx and lured young black people, including those who had been members of gangs. For example, under the leadership of one young African American, Afrika Bambaataa, who was a member of a gang called the

A break dancer headspinning

Black Spades that initially was into drugs and violence, the young people in his area began to focus on graffiti, music,and break dancing. Bambaataa changed the name of his gang to Zulu Nation, and he himself began DJ'ing parties. In 1976, Bambaataa DJ'ed a party for the first time at the Bronx River Community Center. With his group, Soul Sonic Force,

Afrika Bambaataa went on to become a major influence in hip-hop and rap music both in the United States and abroad.

Hip-hop culture encompassed the club and street parties, music, clothes, and break dancing. Music with a strong beat and with breaks to allow a dancer to perform extraordinary moves was required. The dancer needed loose-fitting clothes in which he or she could move easily, and comfortable shoes. Suddenly, young people were wearing baggy pants, loose-fitting shirts, and sneakers. The fashion of baggy pants not only made it easier for a dancer to move, but carried a certain dubious cachet. Although many of the young people wearing them did not realize it, the style "originated in the prisons . . . [where] once behind . . . locked doors prison officials usually remove inmates' belts for obvious reasons. . . . Once these young inmates were released and returned to their old neighborhoods, they brought with them this style of wearing their pants around their hips."[15]

The clothes and music allowed the dancer to move easily and freely, doing a wide variety of sometimes dangerous moves. These included the Moonwalk made popular by Michael Jackson, the Floor Rock, the Handglide or Flow, the Backspin,

the Headspin, the Windmill, and many others.[16]
The Floor Rock, which incorporates two moves
sometimes called Down Rocking and Top
Rocking, is a basic break-dance move in which
the dancer supports himself on one hand and
kicks out with one or both legs, spinning his legs
and body around his supporting hand. The
Handglide allows the dancer to spin his body
while it is balanced on one elbow stuck between
his hips; one hand supports him while the other
hand spins him. In the Backspin, a dancer spins
his body while balanced on his upper back with
his legs tucked up and held by his arms or hands.

The Headspin and the Windmill are two of the
most dangerous moves for a break dancer. In the
Headspin, he spins on his head, using his hands to
spin himself; in the Windmill, the dancer spins his
body on his shoulders and upper back, with legs
spread wide. Each dancer uses a variety of breakdancing moves, but the more original moves he can
devise—and the more dangerous they are—the
more fame he receives.[17]

Break dancers not only danced in clubs to the
music of DJs, they took to the streets with their
boom boxes (or "ghetto blasters," as they were
also called), earning money by performing for

passersby. The money they made was spent on
new outfits to wear for their complex dance routines,
new shoes, and new records or tapes to dance to.
Break dancing often became a dancer's entire life,
and each dreamed of being discovered and hired
to perform on television or in films.

While break dancing was occupying the
energies of many young people, others were working to improve and individualize the music.
Because of the time and skill needed to properly
research, mix, and sample the music, many DJs
were hiring "MCs" to do the rapping, or talking,
each trying to outdo the next with his or her
rhymes, chants, and talk. The DJs, too, were competitive, and looked for newer techniques to make
the music unique. Scratching—moving the record
back and forth in the groove—emerged, as did
"versioning" (mixing old and new music) and sampling. DJs and their MCs added more technical
expertise, expanding their groups—"crews," or
"posses"—and MCs such as Grandmaster Flash
and Kurtis Blow began to draw huge crowds of fans.

Although rap was wildly popular among break
dancers and in the clubs in the cities, it had not
yet broken into the mainstream of American life.
Few radio stations would play rap. Afraid of scaring

away advertisers, and feeling it was a passing fad
that appealed only to a small African American
audience, radio managers, DJs, and record companies shied away from the music. In 1979, however,
one record finally broke though: "Rapper's
Delight" by the Sugarhill Gang, produced by
Sugar Hill Records, a small record company in
Englewood, New Jersey, founded by Sylvia
Robinson. This record went on to sell more than
500,000 copies and become No. 1 on the pop
music charts. It also gave the country the term
hip-hop, a word that was included in the song.
That same year, Grandmaster Flash and the
Furious Five would record "Superrappin'" on the
Enjoy label. After the successes of "Rapper's
Delight" and "Superrappin'," rap music suddenly
became the music of the moment for young
people, spreading beyond the inner city and
across America.

4

Toasts, Boasts, and Snaps

```
I got style, finesse, and a little black book
That's filled with rhymes and I know you wanna look
But the thing that separates you from me
And that is called originality
        — "Rapper's Delight," Sugarhill Gang[1]
```

ALTHOUGH RAP MUSIC GREW FROM
the many musical forms that preceded it, it was
also influenced by a number of nonmusical traditions that, like the music that has evolved over the
centuries, grew out of African traditions. A quick
verbal facility was valued by members of the various
tribes of West Africa, and that appreciation and
skill accompanied the slaves to the United States.
Those verbal skills evolved not only into the call-
and-response technique seen in various types of
black music, but also into the telling of humorous
stories (known as "toasts"), and the quick and witty
taunts known as "snaps" or "playing the dozens."

Humorous storytelling has long been part of
African American culture. Early minstrel shows
often included comedy routines that utilized the

verbal and storytelling abilities of its performers. During the 1920s and '30s, comedy duos such as Harris and Harris ("This is Not the Stove to Brown Your Bread") and Butterbeans and Susie ("Elevator Papa, Switchboard Mama") recited wild, rhyming stories and jokes against a blues background. Later, comedy radio and television shows such as *Amos and Andy*, although they portrayed blacks in a stereotypical manner, were filled with humorous snaps, boasts, and toasts.

As David Toop points out, toasts are narrative poems, "rhyming stories, often lengthy, which are told mostly amongst men. Violent, scatological, obscene, misogynist, they have been used for decades to while away time in situations of enforced boredom, whether prison, armed service, or streetcorner life."[2] In 1953, Willie Dixon and the Big Three Trio recorded "Signifying Monkey," an ancient African rhyming tale. Later, this tradition would be picked up by such rappers as Schoolly-D, whose 1987 "Signifying Rapper" updates this type of tale.

Toasts were and still are used to entertain, but also to insult and taunt another, just as snaps are. Snaps, unlike toasts, are used by both men and women. Both toasts and snaps are a means of gaining admiration from others, and going head-to-head with someone using snaps—playing the dozens—is a battle for respect. The victor, however, aims not merely to win, but to keep his or her opponent from returning fire, and to verbally wipe out that opponent in front of others.

There are many different terms for playing the dozens, including "capping, cracking, bagging, dissing, hiking, joning, ranking, ribbing, serving, signifying, slipping, sounding, and snapping."[3] Although the terms differ, the rules of the game are the same. One person taunts another by teasing or insulting his or her family, playing on words, and painting humorous pictures of them, usually before a crowd who, by its reaction, determines the winner. Because family is important to everyone, attacking a person's family is like a blow to the jaw. Some samples of snaps (short, humorous insulting comments, sometimes in rhyme) that might be used in such a contest include:

```
Your sister is so skinny, her bra fits better
    backward.
Your brother is so ugly, when he sits in the
    sand, the cat tries to bury him.
Your mother is so old, she knew Burger King
    when he was just a prince.
```

Your mother is so cross-eyed, she thinks her
  only child is a twin.
Your mother is so fat, she broke her arm and
  gravy poured out.
Your family is so poor, your mother calls TV
  dinner trays her good china.
Your car is so old, they stole the Club and
  left the car.

Playing the dozens insults an opponent's
family, but a similar game, signifying, insults the
opponent him- or herself using snaps and rhymes.
Some snaps that could be used in signifying are:

You're so dumb, you think Taco Bell is a
  Mexican phone company.
You're so dumb, if you spoke your mind, you'd
  be speechless.
You're so bucktoothed, you can eat corn on
  the cob through a fence.
You're so dumb, you couldn't pass a blood
  test.
You're so stupid, you asked for a price check
  at a 99-cent store.
Your breath smells so bad, people on the
  phone hang up.

Whereas snaps and rhymes are used in playing
the dozens to degrade one's opponent, signifying

could also be used to make someone feel good, and even, as in boasting, to elevate oneself in a verbal contest. Perhaps the most widely publicized boasts are those made by Muhammad Ali when, as Cassius Clay, he faced Sonny Liston in a battle for the World Heavyweight Championship in 1964. Ali entertained and amused audiences with such boasting rhymes as "I float like a butterfly, sting like a bee/Liston will be out in three." Black audiences recognized what Ali was doing, something they themselves did every day: engaging in traditional boasting.

Just as boasting and playing the dozens today are ways of gaining an upper hand over another person, verbal jousts of all kinds are an integral part of African American culture, particularly among boys and men. As Roger D. Abrahams notes, "Verbal contest accounts for a large portion of the talk between members of this group. Proverbs, turns of phrases, jokes, almost any manner of discourse is used, not for purposes of discursive communication but as weapons in verbal battle."[4] Throughout the history of African American music, from ragtime to rap, musicians have drawn upon this tradition extensively, incorporating the spirit of snaps, toasts, and boasts into their songs.

The spirit of competition inherent in boasting and playing the dozens is also present in an art form that directly influenced rap music: graffiti.

Graffiti has existed for thousands of years. When archaeologists unearthed the remains of the city of Pompeii in Italy after it had lain buried in volcanic ash for centuries, they found graffiti scrawled on many of its walls. Since the beginning of history, humans have desired to leave their mark, to be remembered even if only by scratching a message or their initials on a wall. But graffiti assumed the level of an art form in

Graffiti on New York City subway car

New York City in the 1960s and '70s.

During the 1960s, the makeup of the Bronx section of New York changed dramatically. Middle-class white businesses were closing, white families were leaving the Bronx, and poorer black and Hispanic families were moving in. One factor that spurred this exodus was the 1968 completion of a

15,382-unit co-op apartment complex in the Bronx called Co-Op City, housing low- and moderate-income families.[5]

Teenagers from the projects and surrounding slums began forming gangs, and following the usual gang behavior, began to get involved in drugs and violence, but around 1969, another force started to influence them. Graffiti had always been present in New York and the outer boroughs, but at this time, one graffiti artist began signing his graffiti "TAKI 183." TAKI 183 was a teenager from Greece who identified himself using his middle name, Taki, and his street, 183rd. He was widely imitated as other graffiti artist also began to use parts of their names to create nicknames or titles as signatures and to indicate the street numbers where they lived or hung out.

As the craze for graffiti grew, style and artistry became important, and gangs formed whose entire existence revolved around creating graffiti. Even gangs that previously had been into drugs and violence were attracted to the competitive aspects of graffiti writing and drawing. One such gang called itself the Ex-Vandals; another went by the name of the Independent Writers. Both the individuals and the gangs saw graffiti as a competition and as a means of gaining notoriety. However, as Henry A. Rhodes notes, "One could gain respect and recognition by getting one's name around in large quantities, but it was more prestigious to create an original lettering style."[6] Graffiti exhibited the same wild artistic individuality and pride that rap music would soon be expressing. Graffiti artists experimented with their spray-paint cans, trying to create the most original styles. One was an artist known as Super Kool, who widened the dispersion cap on his spray-paint can to get a wider sweep, a technique that was widely imitated by other graffiti artists.[7]

After the city of New York cracked down on graffiti writing in and on the subway trains and the walls of the station platforms by devising a way of washing it off, the graffiti artists branched out to cover buildings and other flat surfaces, creating entire murals that eventually came to be recognized by art dealers as the legitimate artworks they were. In 1980, there was even an art show in Times Square featuring the work of various graffiti artists.

That same year, Richard Goldstein, in an article in the *Village Voice*, defended graffiti artists, and also linked graffiti with rap music. He noted that "graffiti and rap music originated from the same cultural conditions."[8] Both the art of graffiti and the rhythms of rap grew in the inner city among people striving for an artistic expression that captured their experiences. One important contribution graffiti made to rap music, following in the footsteps of the Jamaican DJs, was the tradition and a certain style of naming its artists. Many rappers' names may have evolved from gang names into graffiti signatures, and from there, into the names that became synonymous with rap music itself. Many well-known graffiti artists, such as Phase 2, Futura, and Fab Five Freddy went on to compose rap music.

At the same time that graffiti was becoming noticed and gaining artistic recognition, yet another group was formed that had a definite impact on rap music. This group was born on May 19, 1968, at a birthday celebration in Harlem in honor of Malcolm X (who had been assassinated on February 21, 1965). They called themselves The Last Poets. The Last Poets initially consisted of three poets, Abiodun Oyewole, Alafia Pudim, and Umar Ben Hassan, and a percussionist, Nilaja. They had graduated from the hard-knocks schools of the streets, drug use, and prison, experiences of which they spoke in their poetry. In 1970, they recorded their first record album, *The Last Poets*, with Douglas Records. It consisted of spoken poetry with jazz drumming and instrumentation. Their work combined "revolutionary politics, street language, and percussion in an artistic form that would inspire countless Black Americans."[9] Their performances and records, with poems such as "White Man's Got a God Complex," spoke directly to inner-city young people and would later inspire, in particular, gangsta rappers such as Ice-T and KRS-One.

During the 1960s and early 1970s, the black power movement was growing, but in two directions. Activists such as the Black Panthers, H. Rap Brown (so-called for his verbal facility), and Stokely Carmichael were calling for action with slogans such as "Quit looting and start shooting" and "Burn, baby, burn." On the other hand, Martin Luther King, Jr. and his followers were urging nonviolent protest to initiate change. The assassination of King in 1968 set off a series of riots in major cities across the United States. Many felt that nonviolence had been tried and had failed; now was the time for action, for the assertion of black power and pride. The Last Poets used literary expression to carry this message to people. Accompanied by drums on their records and in their recitations, The Last Poets "painted brutal scenarios of black American life."[10] Their poetry and performances may have been unsettling to some white listeners, but to inner city audiences, their work had the hard ring of truth.

Other poets outside the circle of The Last Poets were also expressing the black experience, although not in such harsh terms. Three of them, Gil Scott-Heron, Nikki Giovanni, and Jayne Cortez, like The Last Poets, combined music with their poetry in an effort to make their message reach their inner-city audiences. Their poetry was highly politicized, painting stark pictures of African American and urban life. As Gil Scott-Heron said in 1972, "Black people everywhere are becoming aware of the gap that exists between American values and the values of our spirits. . . . What we need is self-love and respect. Unfortunately it is not easy to love yourself after years of self-hatred. We see evidence of self-hatred and self-destruction in every city. We must make the extra effort needed to identify the true enemies of our peace and peace of mind."[11] In 1974, Scott-Heron's "The Revolution Will Not Be

Televised" set an example for later rap musicians by presenting a political message against a funky bass-and-rhythm background. Through such poets as Scott-Heron, Cortez, and The Last Poets (and later, Maya Angelou) black urban experience found a poetic release that both uplifted and galvanized audiences in the same ways that rap lyrics and music would.

African American traditions are rich in their variety of artistic expression. Often the simplest thing, such as jumping rope, assumes new meaning when it is interpreted by black American young people. Rap music is only the most recent expression of an artistic tradition that has been passed down without interruption and interpreted in a variety of original ways since early times.

5

raps and rappers

Makin' rap music is our profession
There's only one chance at a first impression
But there are times with records you hear
That out of nowhere seem to catch your ear
   —— "The Greatest Entertainer," Doug E. Fresh[1]

I N MANY WAYS, RAP MUSIC DEFIES
strict categorization. Since it is the expression of a
particular individual's thoughts and ideas, rap
may mix several messages or musical styles
together, do anything the rapper wishes. Today,
however, a listener can loosely classify rap music
into six different styles, which at times may over-
lap and combine: old school rap, gangsta rap,
playa rap, intelligent or message rap, battle rap,
and alternative rap.

The term *old school rap* refers to the style that
emerged in rap's early days, before gangsta and
the other styles began evolving in 1983 with the
release of Run D.M.C.'s "Sucka MC's." Old
school rap is more positive, less political, and less

angry than the rap that began to be produced in
the 1980s. It is the rap of those who pioneered the
music, starting with Kool Herc (Clive Campbell).

As a DJ, Kool Herc would play popular dance
music, throwing in rhymes and sampling from
other records, following the tradition of the DJs
and MCs from Jamaica. Afrika Bambaataa "added
a socially conscious tone to the emerging rap
style. . . . He was rap's most eclectic experimenter,
mixing black dance cuts with tunes from the
whitest of white rock acts, teasing his friends
afterward that he had them dancing to the
Monkees."[2]

Grandmaster Flash (Joseph Saddler), also from
the Bronx, developed rap further by creating
entire narrative poems to accompany the music,
rather than commenting and rhyming only during
appropriate times in the music or to keep the
rhythm going while the DJ changed records.
Grandmaster Flash also began experimenting with
the sound system and with records, trying to
create new sounds. Although a competing DJ,
"Grand Wizard" Theodore Livingston, invented
"scratching" while practicing his raps at home,
Grandmaster Flash and others quickly picked up
on the technique and invented new ones:

I know how to blend. That just came naturally. My main
objective was to take small parts of records and, at first, keep
it on time, no tricks, keep it on time. I'm talking about very
short beats, maybe 40 seconds, keeping it going for about five
minutes, depending on how popular that particular record was.

After that, I mastered punch phrasing—taking certain
parts of a record where there's a vocal or drum slap or a horn. I
would throw it out and bring it back, keeping the other
turntable playing. If this record had a horn in it before the
break came down I would go—BAM, BAM, BAM, BAM-BAM—
just to try this on the crowd.

The crowd, they didn't understand it at first but after a
while it became a thing. After I became popular with it I
wanted to get more popular, but a lot of places where they
heard of me I would ask them if I could get on their turntables.
A few clubs I used to go to, even Disco Fever, they'd say, "No
man, I heard you be scratching up people's records, man. . . ."

A scratch is *nothing* but the back-cueing that you hear in
your ear before you push it out to the crowd. All you have to
know is mathematically how many times to scratch it and when
to let it go—when certain things will enhance the record you're
listening to.[3]

Inner-city African American musicians in
1970s New York were busy with the birth of rap,
creating its vocal styles, and the techniques to
effectively generate and mix the background
sounds. But it was the music of the streets and
clubs. Record companies weren't interested in
what they thought was a strange, passing fad that
appealed to only a small section of their overall

audience. Although in those days, this rap—now called old school rap—was generally enthusiastic and upbeat in both music and message—"flamboyant and fanciful, not violent or sexually explicit"—many felt the music was "too black."[4] Then, in 1979, rap shattered this recording barrier with both The Fatback Band's "You're My Candy Sweet" on Spring Records, the B side of which was a rap called "King Tim III (Personality Jock)," and the Sugarhill Gang's "Rapper's Delight," recorded by Sugar Hill Records. Although The Fatback Band's rap was somewhat popular, it was "Rapper's Delight" that galvanized the industry.

Sugar Hill Records was started by Sylvia

The Sugarhill Gang

Robinson, who was interested in finding new
talent to record. A new sound was in the air—
rap—and more and more, Robinson heard
teenagers talking enthusiastically about MCs and
DJs at various clubs. One day, in a Harlem pizza
parlor, she heard one of the employees either rapping to himself or playing a homemade rap tape
(the story differs). That employee was MC Big
Bank Hank. Interested, Robinson asked him if he
would like to record. Big Bank Hank joined with
two other rappers, and the Sugarhill Gang was
born. The group recorded "Rapper's Delight" at
Robinson's Englewood, New Jersey, studio, and
overnight it seemed, found success. The song sold
more than 500,000 copies and quickly moved to
the No. 1 spot on the pop charts.

"Rapper's Delight" was almost immediately
followed by Kurtis Blow's "Christmas Rappin',"
Grandmaster Flash's "The Message," and numerous other records; in 1981, Disco Daddy and
Captain Rapp's "Gigolo Rap" joined the crowd,
introducing the first West Coast rap. Rap records
and tapes were sellouts, and radio shows were
slowly beginning to recognize and play the music.
At this time, the majority of these records and
tapes were home-produced or produced by small,

independent studios such as Sugar Hill that had formed to answer the demand for rap. Then, in 1983, Run D.M.C. hit the music scene with their "Sucka MC's," and rap broke out of the ghetto.

Run D.M.C. wore hip-hop or street clothes for their performances—warm-up suits, unlaced sneakers, Kangol hats—and their raps were simple. They rapped not only about black experiences as had the old-style rappers, but also about middle-class things such as their shoes. At times, they even changed common nursery rhymes to suit their message. Run D.M.C.'s records took off, selling more than 500,000 copies and going first gold, then platinum. More important, they broke into mainstream America, bringing rap into households that had never before heard such music. Their music drew white fans with their use of heavy metal and rock beats, and both black and

Run D.M.C.

white teens could identify with their lightheartedness and concern for the things that interest all teens: clothes and being cool. This appeal was further strengthened by their collaboration with the rock band Aerosmith in a rap remake of "Walk This Way." Major record companies began seriously looking at rappers and their earning potential, realizing there indeed was a market out there and money to be made. D.M.C. said of the moment when Run D.M.C.'s second single, "Hard Times," hit the pop charts, "I thought, 'We're set.' I knew that nothing could stop us now."[5]

Run D.M.C. led the way not only in popularizing rap with audiences who previously had not heard the music, but in capitalizing on their success. They brought out their own line of "b-boy" clothes, and the Adidas company produced a line of Run D.M.C. shoes. In addition, Run (Joseph Simmons) and D.M.C. (Darryl McDaniels), aided by Jay "Jam Master" Mizell, appeared on *American Bandstand*, on MTV, and at the Grammy Awards, and they acted in two movies, *Krush Groove* and *Tougher Than Leather*.

As the music industry opened up to rap music, Run D.M.C. was joined by other groups and DJs who proved to be equally popular with both black

and white audiences. L. L. Cool J (James Todd
Smith), the grandson of boxing great Muhammad
Ali, found fame with his first single, "I Can't
Live Without My Radio," and Jazzy Jeff and
Fresh Prince (Will Smith) achieved recognition
with their 1988 song "He's the DJ, I'm the
Rapper." Similarly, M. C. Hammer (Stanley Kirk
Burrell) made his first album in the late 1980s,
Feel My Power, which sold 60,000 copies and
led to a record deal with Capitol Records.
Capitol re-released Hammer's album under the
title *Let's Get Started*, and it went on to sell more
than a million and a half copies.

For all their popularity with both black and
white audiences, these groups were criticized by
hard-core rappers for their commercialization of
rap, and for having lost touch with their black
roots. Other rappers made fun of L. L. Cool J's
heavy gold chains and Run D.M.C.'s line of clothing. They had become, many felt, what is now
termed playa rappers, rappers whose only concern
is making money and enjoying the finer things in
life: "Krystal sipping, champagne drinking,
Armani wearing [and] . . . money, mo' money and
mo' money," as Sixth Sense Creations says in a
rap criticizing these groups. Although other rap

styles have become more prominent, playa rap
continues to exist as is seen in the extravagant
lifestyles of such artists as Sean "Puffy" Combs,
Foxy Brown, AZ, Lil' Kim, and even gangsta
rapper Mr. P (Percy Miller), whom *Rap Pages*
named its Man of the Year, in part for his business
skills. According to *Rap Pages*, "*Forbes* [maga-
zine] recognized P's business acumen when they
slated him the tenth most profitable entertainer in
1998. . . . Percy Miller is the businessman who
revolutionized the thinking of securing capital and
controlling the means of production in this rap
industry."[6]

Perhaps in response to this commercialization
of rap, rappers emerged who shunned the glitter
for the message. *Message rap* tried to communicate
the black inner-city experience and warn listeners
about the dangers of drugs and violence. Rappers
such as KRS-One (Kris Parker) and his Boogie
Down Productions saw rap as a way to enlighten
their audience, particularly their younger fans.
Parker ignored the glitz of stardom, promoting
unity and awareness instead, as in his rap, "Illegal
Business," in which he points out that drugs—
cocaine and "ganja"—control not only the ghetto
and keep people down, but control all of America.

Parker raps against the hold that drugs have on black youth in the United States. Young people, he feels, should be aware of how drugs can shape their lives in negative ways.

Although Boogie Down Productions and other rappers such as The Lost Boys, One Million Strong, and ViScOuS refined message rap, rap has been filled with messages since its inception. In 1980, Kurtis Blow recorded two message raps, "The Breaks," and "Hard Times," and Grandmaster Flash had a hit in 1982 with "The Message." Boogie Down Productions and others, though, made message rapping their primary form, addressing political issues in their lyrics in a conscious attempt to educate their listeners about the dangers of the inner-city experience, and using language those listeners could relate to. Many message rappers also attempted to recall for their listeners their heritage and roots in Africa, urging them to feel proud.

Yet another response to playa rap was *militant rap*, which quickly metamorphosed into what is now called gangsta rap. Although rap was popular, few outside of a growing number of both black and white young people around the nation had any idea what rap music was about. Gangsta rap

changed all that; because of its violence and
obscenity, it drew attention to itself and to the
entire rap industry.

On the East Coast, Public Enemy was a no-non-
sense militant rap group with a black nationalistic
message. Public Enemy's organizer, Chuck D
(Carlton Ridenhour) said, "It's about gold brains
now, not gold chains."[7] Public Enemy rapped about
the streets and the political disenfranchisement of
the African American. In their "Fight the Power,"
for example, the group calls out for "brothers and
sisters" to "fight the power," the establishment, to
gain freedom of speech.

Old school and playa rappers, although they
dealt with the black experience, shunned anything
that was greatly controversial, whereas militant rappers such as Public Enemy made controversy their
watchword and were accused of, among other
things, anti-semitism and advocating violence
against women and gays in their raps. Groups such
as Public Enemy rapped hard, politically aware
lyrics and went to the edge, but they didn't step
over; it took the gangsta rappers to do that.

In 1988, N.W.A. (Niggaz With Attitude) burst
on the rap scene with their "Straight Outta
Compton." Gangsta rap was born. The term

gangsta rap had been coined around 1987. Some
hip-hoppers, mainly from the East Coast, feel that
Philadelphia's Schoolly D was the original gangsta
rapper, but the genre was christened with Ice-T's
album *Rhyme Pays*, and came to maturity with
N.W.A.'s 1988 album. Gangsta rap is harsh, hard-
hitting, brutal, bloody, and usually obscene. It
exaggerates the macho myths of the 1970s blaxploitation movies, and its lyrics deal with guns,
gang wars, treacherous females, drugs, alcohol,
and going against "the man" (the police).

Spoken against a heavy bass-and-drum background, with its noise and violent lyrics gangsta
rap was disturbing to the white American establishment. N.W.A.'s "F— the Police" resulted in
the F.B.I.'s sending letters to police chiefs nation-
wide, warning that the rap was agitating against
law enforcement and its officials. N.W.A.'s album
was soon joined by others from such South Central
Los Angeles rappers as Ice Cube (O'Shea Jackson,
who was originally a member of N.W.A.), Too
Short, the Geto Boys, Eazy-E (Eric Wright), and
Ice-T, all describing the underside of ghetto existence with its gang warfare, drug dealing, and con-
stant threat of death. As DJ Easy Mo Bee said of
them, "You got to give [credit] to a lot of these

gangsta rappers. They are talking about hard social issues. They are angry, and this is the only voice they have."[8]

Gangsta rap not only disturbed the public, it drew attention to itself and the entire field of rap music when, in 1990, in Florida, the group 2 Live Crew was charged with obscenity. On June 8 of that year, the owner of a Florida record store was arrested for selling the group's album *As Nasty As They Wanna Be*. Two days later, after a live performance, the members of 2 Live Crew were themselves arrested, and the group's leader, Luther Campbell, was charged with obscenity. During the 2 Live Crew trial, Dr. Henry Gates, Jr., a scholar of African American studies, testified that the music the group was creating was part of an oral tradition stretching back to an Africa in which society and its elements were criticized, often harshly. Although this and other

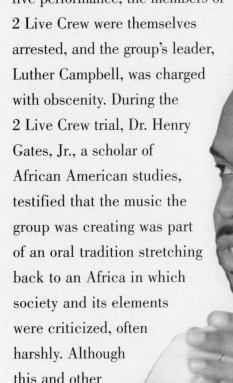

Luther Campbell

testimony led to the acquittal of 2 Live Crew, the
arrest and trial stirred controversy about how far
music for young people should be allowed to go.
Earlier, in 1985, in reaction to explicit lyrics of all
types, Tipper Gore, wife of Al Gore, who would
later be elected vice president under Bill Clinton,
had founded the Parents Music Resource Center
(PMRC) to promote responsibility and self-policing
in the recording industry. Spurred by the controversy of the 2 Live Crew trial, the PMRC wanted
to subject records to a rating system, but both
artists and recording industry companies objected.
Although protested by various artists, a compromise
was reached when the recording industry agreed
to label certain tapes and CDs as having "Explicit
Lyrics," and marking them with a "Parental
Advisory."

Despite the PMRC, and congressional hearings
on gangsta rap in 1994, the gangsta rappers continued to compose explicit, hard-hitting lyrics, but
their case for artistic freedom was not helped by the
behavior of some of their members. Snoop Doggy
Dogg, Slick Rick, and 2Pac not only rapped about
crime, but were accused of living their lyrics. In
1993, Snoop Doggy Dog was accused of possession
of an unlicensed weapon, and later, of being an

accessory to murder. The next year, Tupac Shakur (2Pac) was robbed and shot in midtown Manhattan. Later, Shakur, after a drawn-out East Coast–West Coast feud with Notorious B.I.G. (Christopher Wallace), was murdered in Las Vegas. It was thought that his assailants may have been affiliated with Notorious B.I.G., who, on March 9, 1997, was himself gunned down in a drive-by shooting. In 1998, Ol' Dirty Bastard seemed to be on a one-man crime spree. According to *Rap Pages*,

Snoop Doggy Dogg

Between interrupting the Grammys ("Wu-Tang is for the children"), getting shot (during a robbery at a Brooklyn apartment), checking out of the hospital against doctor's orders (after being shot), shoplifting (a pair of $50 Nikes in Virginia), being wanted on outstanding warrants (for shoplifting), failing to pay child support (for some of his 13 children), recording cameos on hit singles . . . getting arrested (for allegedly threatening to kill security guards at a Los Angeles nightclub) and changing his name yet again (to Big Baby Jesus), ODB certainly stayed busy.[9]

That same year, some of the violence in rap music seemed to run over into real life as rappers took on the media. Female teenage rap sensation Foxy Brown, although not a gangsta rapper, confronted *Vibe* magazine editor-in-chief Danyel Smith about a *Vibe* cover that showed Brown practically nude. Upset about the cover, she allegedly struck Smith. In November of that same year, Deric (D-Dot) Angelettie, angered by a photograph in *Blaze* magazine (the parent publication of *Vibe*), went to the magazine's offices with three friends and confronted editor-in-chief Jesse Washington. According to Washington, they threw him to the ground, and "started kicking me and hitting me with chairs."[10] Angelettie and one of those with him were arrested for assault. In 2000, Sean "Puffy" Combs, rap artist and recording entrepreneur, was charged with carrying a concealed weapon and with possession of an unlicensed firearm after pulling a gun outside a New York nightclub. It seemed that many rappers wanted to play out the crimes about which they sang.

Some gangsta rappers, however, tried to bring their messages to ever-greater numbers not with illegal activities, but with their records—and in film. With the success of black film producers such as Spike Lee and John Singleton, rap moved beyond the recording industry. Rappers provided the background scores for such movies as *Do the Right Thing* and *Boyz N the Hood*, the latter also featuring gangsta rapper Ice-Cube, who displays a remarkable talent for acting in the film, and who went on to co-star in *Three Kings* with George Clooney in 1999.

Gangsta rap remained alive and well at the turn of the century, with older rappers such as Ice Cube and Ice-T being joined by newer, hard-core rappers such as Busta Rhymes (Trevor Smith), who, in his 1998 release *Extinction Level Event*, made dire apocalyptic predictions about the year 2000.

Confrontation has always been a part of rap music, but unlike the real-life, often criminal confrontations of the gangsta rappers, it usually takes the more peaceable form of a verbal war for supremacy: *battle rap*. Just as griots competed with one another, and Jamaican MCs and their sound systems had battles to determine which was the best, rappers have engaged in battle rap since rap's beginnings. When rap was the music of the streets, two MCs might compete in a park, playground, or club, "kicking their rhymes freestyle"—off the tops of their heads—to determine who was the best.[11] After record companies began recording rap, battles would take the form of one MC or group "answering" a cut on another group's record. Battle rap involves a great deal of both toasting and boasting, as well as throwing out rhymed snaps against one's opponent. In many ways, battle rap stands outside the individual styles of rap; it is something any rapper, whether old school, message, gangsta, or playa, might engage in at some time or another. It is a tradition rather than a style.

Many contemporary rappers are breaking out of the old school, playa, message, or gangsta molds and are engaged in creating yet another form of rap music, which, for want of a better term, has been called *alternative rap*. Alternative rap artists go beyond merely sampling rhythm and blues or jazz.

They incorporate these and other musical styles more fully into their compositions. In 1993, Guru and the Digable Planets brought together hip-hop and jazz in their album *Reachin' (A New Refutation of Time and Space)*. The result, as Christopher John Farley points out, "is a whimsical delight, delivering the shock of the new by evoking the glory of the old. . . . [The] jazzy undercurrents give the album a laid-back quality that refutes the riotous stereotype of rap."[12] Although Ismail, the group's leader, denied doing alternative rap, fearing the criticism that their music would be viewed as "soft," the album helped set standards for alternative rap.

Alternative encompasses many different types of music. For example, in a November 16, 1998, *Newsweek* article, "Method to the Madness," N'Gai Croal hailed Wu-Tang Clan as having created a new sound, "hard-core soul." "With this record," Croal says, "Meth [Method Man (Clifford Smith), the MC of Wu-Tang] has created a new strain of rap, a gritty soulful sound. . . . He uses his lyrical genius to plunge us into a mind-state as chaotic as the paranoid stream of consciousness of a James Ellroy narrator. . . . Call it hard-core soul; rugged for the fellas, yet smooth enough for the ladies."[13]

Method Man and Wu-Tang Clan were doing what a
great many rappers of the late 1990s were doing,
including Guru and Digable Planets. They were

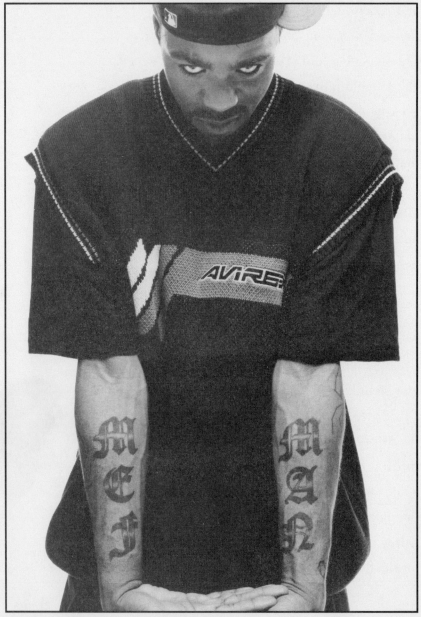

Method Man

reinventing the music yet again, creating alternatives to "traditional" rap.

One alternative artist who shone in 1998 and 1999 was Lauryn Hill. *Time* magazine praised her 1998 release, *The Miseducation of Lauryn Hill*, saying,

> Hill has given hip-hop the gift of her own heart: bruised, but still beating strong. She has shown that the genre can reach down deeper than bravado, deeper than rage, and dare to reveal an artist's emotional insecurities and romantic failing and then transform those feelings into music that's eloquent and universal.[14]

New York magazine was equally effusive in its praise of Hill and her album, saying that it "dances gracefully among straight rap, reggae-tinged head-bobbers, and deliciously funky soul."[15]

The Roots' 1999 release *Things Fall Apart* also combines old and new. As in Hill's album, the Roots use less sampling and return "to the old school of rap with their live band sound and their midtempo beats."[16] The emotions of the music, however, are not those of rage and anger as was so often the case in the 1980s. "You Got Me," one of its best tracks, is a love song featuring Erykah Badu. This combining of old and new with a heightened personal consciousness has great appeal with both black and white audiences.

In a similar manner, Wyclef Jean of the Fugees created a solo album in 1997, *Wyclef Jean Presents the Carnival Feat, Refugee Allstars*, that brilliantly merges 1970s pop music with contemporary rap. In 1998, *Rap Pages* said he "clearly comprehends that Hip-Hop is interchangeable with practically any form of music."[17] The fact that such alternative rap is popular with listeners was proven when Wyclef Jean's album went platinum in November 1997 soon after its release.

Twenty years ago, rap existed only on the streets and in the clubs of New York City; by the end of the twentieth century, the Grammy Awards had established a rap category, and rap had gone mainstream and worldwide in its appeal. The music, however, continues to be that of youth and protest, and it continues to evolve. With the kinds of transformations rap has undergone since its inception, it is difficult to predict where it will go. All one can say is that it will, indeed, go somewhere new and interesting— and, perhaps, controversial.

6

queendoms of rap

```
Give me body (Don't make me wait)
Welcome into my queendom
Come one, come all
'Cause when it comes to lyrics, I bring them
In spring I sing, in fall I call
I've prepared a place on my dance floor
The time is now for you to party
You to move (One Nation Under the Groove)
    —— "Come into My House," Queen Latifah[1]
```

RAP MUSIC HAS MAINLY BEEN SEEN AS
the province of men and boys, but women have
always played a significant part in African oral
tradition and in African American life. Many
griots were women, and throughout the centuries,
women have played active roles both as performers and as activists. During the twentieth
century, for example, poets such as Gwendolyn
Brooks, Nikki Giovanni, and Maya Angelou
have become the poetic voices of black women
everywhere, and Rosa Parks, in her quiet protest
against segregated busing, proved to be an

important catalyst in the civil rights movement in America. In music, Ella Fitzgerald was the queen of scat, and the Supremes set the soul music standard for girl groups in the 1960s and '70s. One female performer who was a direct forerunner of rap was Shirley Ellis. Her wordplay songs were extremely popular among both black and white audiences, including "The Name Game," in which a word game is chanted (rapped) against a beat.

When rap music was just beginning to break out of inner city neighborhoods, women rappers were starting to shape their music. One of the first rappers, although she is often forgotten, was Sheila Spencer. Better known for her portrayal of Thomasina on NBC's soap opera *Another World*, Spencer began rapping under the names She and Ms. D.J. in the early 1980s. She had sung in a choir in Brooklyn from childhood, had provided background vocals for Kurtis Blow's first album, and had been a boxing cheerleader for Muhammad Ali, doing rhyming cheers.[2] In an attempt to bring a female rapper into the market, Clapper records released a single, "Ms. D.J. Rap It Up!" in the early 1980s. Although Spencer's single gained some popularity, and other women rappers such as

Sula and Lady B also made recordings, and the girl
group Sequence hit the charts in 1980 with their
"Simon Says," female rappers didn't become big-
time until the advent of Roxanne Shanté.

Roxanne Shanté (Lolita Gooden) was hard,
tough, and "built a career around telling black men
where to get off."[3] As in traditional call-and-
response, Shanté was loudly answering the implicit
and explicit challenges in many of the raps by men.
In 1984, in response to UTFO's "Roxanne,
Roxanne," Shanté made her first single, "Roxanne's
Revenge." The rap was "profane, independent, and
bodacious. She dissed the UTFO crew with the
kind of verbal backhand that was usually displayed
by male MCs."[4] For female rap fans, her single was
revolutionary: finally, here was someone standing
up to the brothers and going them one better. In her
"Have a Nice Day," for example, Shanté humorously takes on the top male groups of the day:

```
Now I'm not out to dis the whole Boogie Down
Just a featherweight crew from that part
    of town
Ya made a little record and then you start
    frontin'
Tried to blank the Juice Crew but ain't
    hear nuthin'
```

Now KRS-One, you should go on vacation
With a name soundin' like a wack radio station
And as for Scott La Rock, you should be
    ashamed
When T La Rock said "It's yours"
He didn't mean his name
So step back poppin' all that junk
Or else BDP will stand for broken down punks
'Cause I'm an all-star, just like Julius
    Irving
And Roxanne Shanté is only good for steady
    servin'
I'm Shanté, I'm-I'm Shanté
I'm Shanté, I'm and your rhymes rh-rhymes
    are dead[5]

Having forcibly broken the ice, Roxanne
Shanté was quickly followed by other female
rappers. Some chose only to cash in on Shanté's
success, calling themselves "Roxanne's Doctor,"
"The Real Roxanne," and "Roxanne's
Psychiatrist." Other groups, such as BWP
(Bitches With Problems), directly attacked men's
macho attitudes, and the popular Salt-n-Pepa
(Cheryle James and Sandi Denton), with DJ Dee
Dee "Spinderella" Roper (who replaced DJ
Latoya Hanson), created sassy, provocative raps.
    Cheryle James and Sandi Denton met while

enrolled at Queensborough Community College. A
friend, Herby "Luvbug" Azor, had to produce a
record for a class he was attending at the Center of
Media Arts. Azor wrote a rap response to the record
"The Show" by Doug E. Fresh and Slick Rick and
called it "The Showstopper (Is Stupid Fresh)." He
asked James and Denton if they would perform it,
and they recorded it under the group name Super
Nature. The record earned Azor an A in his class
and was later picked
up by Pop Art
Records, which
released it in
October 1985. After
its moderate suc-
cess, James and
Denton were signed
by Next Plateau
Records and
became Salt-n-Pepa.

Salt-n-Pepa

Although Salt-n-
Pepa were and still
are very successful,
many feminists have
criticized them and other female rappers for a lack
of feminist sensibility. Queen Latifah, on the other

9 1

hand, has become a spokeswoman for feminism and nationalism in her raps. Queen Latifah (Dana Owens) was born in East Orange, New Jersey. When she was only eight years old, a cousin named her Latifah, a name she kept. As Latifah was growing up, rap was beginning to become popular, and she and two friends in high school formed a group they called "Ladies Fresh," rapping for fun. Then another high school rap group challenged them to a battle. "We stayed up all night writing stuff," Latifah recalled, "and I haven't stopped since."[6] After the competition, which they won, the group made a demo tape and sent it to MTV host Fab Five Freddy, who, after listening to it, took it to Tommy Boy records, which immediately signed Latifah. Latifah says her raps are "for guys to understand and for ladies to be proud of."[7]

Queen Latifah was something new on the rap scene: a woman who spoke up for all women, and a woman who did not fit the flygirl image most female rappers had at that time. She had dark skin, was heavier than most female pop singers, and had short hair. She didn't attack men in her compositions, nor was she encouraging a provocative attitude toward them. She rapped about black nationalism and the plight of women. As Maurice

K. Jones says, "Latifah was the *griotte* to Shanté's gossipmonger. . . . Latifah called for unity and dignity."[8] In her "The Evil That Men Do," for example, Latifah paints a poignant portrait of the problems black women face, the problems of being on welfare and without decent housing, subject to the whims of faceless bureaucrats, in "no man's land."[9]

Despite the moderate success of two albums, *All Hail the Queen* in 1989 and *Nature of a Sista* in 1991, Tommy Boy Records did not re-sign her. In 1993, however, her album *Black Reign*, produced by Motown Records, earned her a gold record. Like many male rappers such as Ice-Cube and Will Smith, Queen Latifah has gone on to become successful and well known on television in the show *Living Single*, and in film (*House Party 2*, *Juice*, and *Set It Off*), proving herself a talented actress and comedienne. An astute business-woman, she also founded Flavor Unit, a management and record company that has produced such hip-hop acts as Apache and Blacksheep.

At the same time that Queen Latifah was gain-ing fame as a musician and actress, another female rapper was achieving a more dubious kind of fame. In 1992, Sister Souljah (Lisa Williamson),

a self-proclaimed "raptivist" from New York and
New Jersey, was promoting her album *360 Degrees
of Power*. In an interview with the *Washington
Post*, Souljah was asked about the thinking behind
a recent truce between L.A.'s main rival gangs, the
Crips and the Bloods. They asked themselves, she
said, "If black people kill black people everyday,
why not have a week and kill white people? . . . So
if you're a gang member and you would normally
be killing somebody, why not kill a white
person?"[10] Bill Clinton, who was then running for
president, publicly attacked her comment at Jesse
Jackson's National Rainbow Coalition convention
in Washington. "Those remarks," said Clinton,
were "filled with the kind of hatred that you do
not honor today."[11] Although Clinton's comments
angered Jackson, they proved a temporary boon
for the militant Sister Souljah, who until then had
had a rather low-key career. After a spate of talk
show appearances in connection with all the com-
motion, however, Sister Souljah was not heard
from again until 1995, when she published a
book, *No Disrespect*, dealing with the relationship
between African American men and women.[12] In
1999, her first novel, *The Coldest Winter Ever*, was
published by Pocket Books. The novel tells of a

young woman, Santiaga Winter, and her life. Souljah deals with basic concerns of African Americans and conveys the message that black men and women must support one another.

As the 1990s progressed, raps by women changed from the feminist messages of Queen Latifah and the militancy of Sister Souljah to ones that reveled in materialism and sex with such rappers as Foxy Brown and Lil' Kim. Although in 1999, Foxy Brown produced an album that muted the "sex kitten" role she had adopted in her first album, her feminist messages are weak compared with those of Queen Latifah.

Foxy Brown (Inga Marchand) sang sexy, provocative raps on her first album, *Foxy Ill Na Na*, which went platinum. Taking her name from Pam Grier's classic blaxploitation superheroine, she captivated audiences with her "tough, trashy talk and thongs-and-ice look. . . . Brown's image was part 'ho, part gun moll. Wrapped in furs, constantly deferring to male patrons, and luxury-obsessed, she wasn't doing much for any . . . socialist feminist animal rights–activist causes."[13] In her second album, released in 1999, *Chyna Doll*, Brown tried to change this image. As Evelyn McDonnell said in her review of the album, "She wants us to see her as an individual with her own particular story, not a celestial being."[14] In *Chyna Doll*, Brown laments the loneliness of life at the top, and the friends she has lost, and attempts to convey a feminist message about the hardships of growing up as a black woman. The music is skilled and the songs appealing, but considering her past albums, the message is a bit weak.

Lil' Kim, former friend of Foxy Brown and former girlfriend of Notorious B.I.G., produced an album, *Hardcore*, with X-rated rhymes set in the bedroom, at parties, and even in the movie theater. The album was an immediate success, "making the highest ever debut entry by a female rapper on the Billboard chart."[15] As with others in rap, Kim then turned businesswoman and actress, appearing in the film *She's All That*, and in 1998, forming Queen Bee Records. But Foxy Brown and Lil' Kim's appeal extended beyond film and music, resulting in numerous sites on the internet filled with provocative pictures of each.

While sexy rappers lured and enticed their audiences with X-rated promises, other women were busy making more lasting contributions to the evolution of rap and hip-hop. Missy Elliott (Melissa

Elliott), who had begun her musical career as part of
the trio Sista and then gone on to writing, produc-
ing, and guesting on a number of rhythm and blues
hits, brought out her hit single "The Rain (Supa
Dupa Fly)" in 1997. The follow-up album, *Supa
Dupa Fly*, which had cameos by Lil' Kim, Busta
Rhymes, and Da Brat, was also a success. It was a
"sleekly distinctive mix of syncopated beats, judi-
cious samples, outright pop hooks, and Elliott's ono-
matopoeic stream-of-consciousness rhymes."[16] *Supa
Dupa Fly* mixed rapping and rhythm and blues
singing to create a new kind of sound. *Rap Pages*
magazine listed her in their "Noize Makers of
1998," saying, "Missy' Elliott is one of the most
gifted talents on the music scene
today. She manages herself,
recently started her own
label, Gold Mine Records,

Missy
Elliott

produces, writes, and creates highly innovative and entertaining videos."[17]

Another artist who shook up rap in the late 1990s was Lauryn Hill, one of the most influential figures in alternative rap. Hill grew up in South Orange, New Jersey, and was interested in singing and performing from the time she was a child. While she was still in high school, Hill won a recurring role on the television soap opera *As The World Turns*, and in 1993 played a troubled teen in *Sister Act 2*. In addition to her acting, while in high school, Hill formed a rap group, the Fugees (refugees), whose first album, *Blunted on Reality*, did poorly, although a second album, *The Score*, was a hit, selling more than 17 million copies worldwide.[18]

When *The Score* hit big, Hill dropped out of Columbia University, where she had been going to school, and began exploring what she could do solo. Needing inspiration, she went to Jamaica, where she was allowed to record in the studio of reggae superstar Bob Marley (Hill was engaged to his son, Rohan Marley, with whom she has two children). After a great deal of work, her hit album *The Miseducation of Lauryn Hill* came out in 1998. An enticing blend of rap, reggae, rhythm

and blues, and rock, the album earned Hill ten
Grammy nominations and five Grammy Awards.
By the end of the 1990s, Hill had her own production company, was touring, and had ideas about a
multitude of projects, including the possibility of
making black science-fiction films. Realizing the
influence a singer of her stature can have as a role
model and as a voice for change, Hill said in
1999, "There are kids in the audiences now who
weren't born when there wasn't hip-hop. . . . They
grew up on it; it's part of the culture. It's a huge
thing. It's not segregated anymore. It's not just in
the Bronx; it's all over the world. That's why I
think it's more crucial now that we, as artists, take
advantage of our platform."[19]

One '90s group, TLC, incorporates some of the
raunch of Foxy Brown's first album, yet experi-
ments with different music styles similar to
Lauryn Hill's. TLC consists of Tionne "T-Boz"
Watkins, Lisa "Left Eye" Lopes, and Rozonda
"Chilli" Thomas. With their first album,
CrazySexyCool, the group found an audience
among both black and white rap fans. Their
second album, FanMail, produced in 1999,
attempted to build on that audience and also to
move in new musical directions. "Unpretty," one

song on the album, moves in a rock direction, whereas "Come On Down" shifts the group, unpredictably, toward country-pop.

When hip-hop and rap began, the music mainly accompanied young black kids rapping on playgrounds and in clubs, and boys break dancing on the streets to the throbbing sounds of boom boxes. At the beginning of the twenty-first century, rap is now recognized as a valid form of music, and with the help of its talented artists, particularly women such as Lauryn Hill and Missy Elliott, and those in TLC, it will continue to evolve and speak to young people around the world.

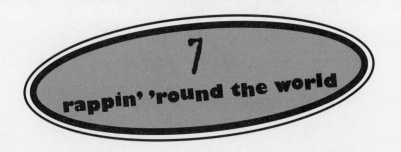

```
Take heed 'cause I'm a lyrical poet
Miami's on the scene just in case you didn't know it
My town, that created all the bass sound
Enough to shake and kick holes in the ground
'Cause my style's like a chemical spill
Feasible rhymes that you can vision and feel
    — "Ice, Ice Baby," Vanilla Ice[1]
```

aS RAP BECAME MORE POPULAR,
white rappers and rap groups emerged. Just as
white musicians had adopted ragtime, blues,
jazz, rhythm and blues, and rock 'n' roll, young
white musicians were attracted to rap not only
for its musical potential but because of its anti-
establishment posture, its protest, and its coolness. For the most part, black rappers felt that
such groups cheapened the genre or were phonies,
having had none of the African American or
inner-city experiences on which the music was
built. Even such groups as 3rd Bass, made up of
Pete Nice, MC Serch, and black DJ Richie Rich,
they felt, failed to equal rap music as it is played

by black rappers, although they earned some respect from black rappers because all three had grown up in New York City surrounded by black culture. The problem, as perceived by black rappers, was not one of color, however, but one of cultural heritage.

One significant difference between white and black rappers in the United States is the subjects of their raps. Whereas the majority of black rappers deal with the horrors or pleasures of black experience, white rappers either try to imitate this, or rap of things that might seem shallow by comparison. In the case of the Beastie Boys, this has often taken the form of rapping about partying and

The Beastie Boys

drinking beer. One result has been that many black artists and critics feel the Beastie Boys and similar white rappers were making fun of black culture by imitating the style of black rappers.

Vanilla Ice (Robbie Van Winkle), one of the first white rappers to hit the pop charts, attempted to imitate black raps in his own lyrics, saying they were drawn from his own experiences. In his interviews with the press, he told of a life that supported this view. He said that he had grown up knowing hardship, attending a tough, inner-city Miami high school as a classmate of Luther Campbell of 2 Live Crew, and that he had been stabbed in a gang fight. He went on to achieve fame when he became one of the opening acts for M. C. Hammer's "U Can't Touch This" 1990 tour, but once he was in the spotlight, Van Winkle's background didn't hold up to research. A journalist exposed Van Winkle as having grown up as a middle-class kid in Carrollton, Texas. Once this came out, the hip-hop community dropped him like

Vanilla Ice

a hot potato, and he was condemned by critics as a "bare-faced counterfeit."[2] By 1999, Van Winkle was attempting to resurrect his failed musical career, playing in clubs in Canada.

The Beastie Boys never presumed to be anything but what they were—middle-class Jewish kids from the suburbs. White fans enthusiastically took to their rambunctious lyrics advocating the party life, and their first album, *License to Ill*, became the biggest-selling rap album of the time. The Beastie Boys' one mistake was a pornographic scratch single, "Cookie Puss," a so-called "punk rap" record—a type critic David Toop calls "a hilarious multiple pile-up of heavy metal, synthesizer rock, and hip-hop."[3] Because of its implicit mockery of black rap in its use of the style employed by many black rappers, "Cookie Puss" is one of the reasons many felt the Beastie Boys were making fun of black culture in their music.

More recently, white Detroit rapper Eminem (Marshall Mathers) found success doing his version of gangsta rap. His 1999 album *Slim Shady* sold nearly a million copies within a few weeks of its release. Music critic David E. Thigpen of *Newsweek* said of the album,

Not since the heyday of N.W.A. has hip-hop served up a feast of violence and fantasy as fiendishly witty. . . . On a song titled *'97 Bonnie & Clyde*, a ripping satire of Will Smith's treacly *Just the Two of Us*, Eminem raps about pushing his troublesome spouse off a pier while their daughter looks on. "There goes mama splashing in the water/ No more fighting with dada/ No more restraining order." Edgy stuff, even by rap standards.[4]

Eminem, while a success, is still conscious of the fact that the "greats" of rap are African

Eminem

American, and feels that because of his skin color many may not listen seriously to his music: "Some people only see that I'm white."[5] Christopher John Farley of *Time*, in reviewing Eminem's *The Marshall Mathers LP*, released in 2000, observes, however, that "The old take on white rappers . . . was that they were, for the most part, whites who wanted to be black. But the new breed of white rappers—guys like Eminem, Kid Rock and the punkish Bloodhound Gang—is proudly white, and they tell you all about it in their songs."[6]

Eminem explores his own life—an odd and violent one, as evidenced by such songs as "Kill You" on his *The Marshall Mathers LP* album—as do many other white rappers. Kid Rock, who travels with a six-foot bodyguard and rapping midget Joe C., spouts what is often called "Trailer-trash hip-hop," a mix of hip-hop and trailer rock. As he says, "When hip-hop came in, so many white kids wanted to be part of that culture, start wearing their hat sideways, using a little Ebonics. I thought it's cool to like hip-hop, but it's also cool to be white."[7]

When a musical form seems to embody all that a young generation is seeking—rebellion, hipness or coolness, protest—and is also almost universally despised by the older generation, it is only to be expected that those young people will claim the music as their own, whether they are listeners or musicians, black, white, Latino, European, or Asian. Just as many white young people in the United States found the voice of their generation in the rap music coming out of the inner cities of America, young people around the world have found in rap a global expression of their time.

In 1992, Jay Cocks wrote in *Time*,

> Rap, which began as a fierce and proudly insular music of the American black underclass, is now possibly the most successful American export this side of the microchip, permeating, virtually dominating, worldwide youth culture. It is both a recreational vehicle and a form of social commentary. . . . The language may differ from place to place, even when it's English, but the music is everywhere—in the air, on the streets, in the racks.[8]

In Europe, as in the United States, rap is a music, a lifestyle, and a fashion. The baggy pants, expensive sneakers, hooded sweatshirts, and jewelry of the hip-hop culture are everywhere. Young people in various European countries imitate the gangs of U.S. cities, creating posses that provide the same support one might find in a gang or in a family. And European young people dance to, listen to, and compose the music that goes with these fashions and styles. There are two reasons for the large number of European rappers. First, the music is a music of youth. More practically, when compared with conventional recordings, a rap album can be recorded quickly at home, with cheap equipment.

In the late 1970s, rap began to filter into England in the form of cheaply made, often homemade tapes, but the music did not formally reach Europe until 1982, when Afrika Bambaataa and his Fab Five Freddy made a European tour that began in London. Before Bambaataa's tour, break dancing had become popular both in England and on the Continent. After his tour, European teens began to go further, imitating American rapping, organizing parties, and rapping in English.

When Afrika Bambaataa made his tour, according to Marie-Agnés Beau of France, he gave "strength to the whole hip-hop movement, structured around the Zulu Nation, with its rules, its hierarchy and . . . nonviolent spirit: [hip-hop] grew up as a big and strong family."[9] Following the example of Bambaataa and other American rappers who also began to perform in England and Europe, rap gained in popularity and began to change, adapting to each individual country.

In England, where minorities were already well represented vocally by such artists as Caribbean dub poet Linton Kwesi Johnson, rap was absorbed by the club scene and eventually evolved into "trip-hop," a kind of slow dance rap with more sullen lyrics than the louder lyrics of protest found in American rap. Trip-hop originated in Bristol, England, and came to public attention with the release of the album *Blue Lines* by Massive Attack in 1991. It "incorporated satellite rappers and vocalists, simmering beats, dub bass, and string arrangements into a groundbreaking vision."[10] Massive Attack was soon followed by the album *Maxinquaye* by the singer Tricky (Adrian Thaws). In this album, Tricky redid two of Public Enemy's songs, "Black Steel in the Hour of Chaos" and "Suffocated Love," as well as including his own compositions, and establishing the features that have come to characterize trip-hop:

> The fundamental trip-hop tempo is slow, slow but relentless, presided over by immense bass figures, as deep but less booming than those of house music. There are lots of rhythm drop-outs, as in dub, and inserted snippets of instruments or noises proliferate wildly in the cleverest mixes. The tone of many trip-hop numbers is sleepy, jaded, but the lyrics . . . spring, likely as not, from the raw wounds of social and romantic anguish.[11]

Whereas trip-hop is coolly angry, another type of music in England, ragga, also derived from American rap, is a more in-your-face style. As Jay Cocks of *Time* describes ragga, "It sounds like reggae on mega-vitamins, bulked-up and bass-pummeled, and it has its origins both in the Caribbean and in an aggressive black awareness."[12]

In other countries, initially, rappers merely imitated the American rappers, rapping in English. French rapper MC Solaar, who was born in Africa, said, "Parisian rap is pretty much a U.S. branch office. We copy everything, don't we? We don't even take a step back."[13] In France, *le rap* didn't progress until rappers began rapping in their own language. Although less violent than American rap, French rap had its own message and was pleasing to its audience. As Marie-Agnés Beau

MC Solaar

points out, "Rap in French flowed spontaneously, sounded good, and was much more explicit than in English."[14] One of the first hits in French, "Auteuil Neuilly Passy," by Les Inconnus (the Unknowns) ridicules and criticizes the wealthy who live in the rich sections of Paris.

MC Solaar, quickly emerged as the first star in French rap, singled out not only for his messages, but "because of his very open and positive attitude, his strong literary talents and humour."[15] Besides rapping in French rather than English, Solaar avoided all use of American slang in his raps. Because of this, the French government, which continually strives to keep the French language "pure," has endorsed Solaar's brand of hip-hop. Although he addresses social problems, as do American rappers, Solaar also composes raps that are highly contemplative and philosophical. In the cover notes of his "La fin justifie les moyens" (The End Justifies the Means), he says,

> I got into this track totally differently because I used to study philosophy at school. . . . I [was] thinking of Nietzsche, the German philosopher. So I go with one of his theories and I develop and develop and develop to say that the end justifies the means, but sometimes we have to question "Do I do the right thing to have this?"[16]

MC Solaar made his American debut in a
cameo appearance on Guru's album *Jazzmatazz*, in
1992. In 1994, his own album, *Prose Combat*, was
released in the United States as well as elsewhere
around the world.

In Italy, rap got off to a slow start; however,
what has emerged is strongly rooted in ideology.
The rapper Jovanotti is credited with having
begun rap in Italy. His initial raps were simple,
but soon evolved to reflect a more radical political
stance. In Italy, rappers congregate in social
groups called posses that, as one rapper said, try
to express "the disease of Italian society."[17] The
raps created by these groups and by individual
rappers are becoming more hard-core, more angry,
although, as Marie-Agnés Beau notes, there is no
gangsta rap in Europe, the various rap groups
keeping closer to Afrika Bambaataa and his Zulu
Nation's message of social responsibility, culture,
and peace.

Rap has spread to every European country,
into the former Soviet Union, and even into South
America and Japan. In Brazil, for example, rap is
tinged with samba rhythms, but its message is still
one of protest and violence. In fact, in 1992, one
of its most popular songs, "I'm Happy (I Killed the

President)," by a rapper called Gabriel the Thinker, was forced off the radio by the Brazilian government. In it, Gabriel describes how he would assassinate former President Fernando Collor.

In Japan, rap has achieved almost a cult status and is seen as emblematic of protest by the younger generation against the rigid older Japanese establishment. Japanese youth who are into rap are fascinated by everything having to do with black culture. According to *Time*'s Jay Cocks, they even attempt to look black: "rap-blitzed kids can invest seven hours and from $324 to $1,215 at a hair salon" to have their hair arranged in dreadlocks. In addition, they go to tanning salons "with names like 'Neo-Blackers' and mail-order skin-darkeners like 'African Special' ($315 a one-month supply)."[18]

Rappers in Japan dress in the hip-hop style, wearing unlaced sneakers and warm-up suits, and rap in both English and Japanese. For the most part, however, their raps lack the violence and outrage of American rap, and in comparison, sometimes sound lightweight—or even silly. Takagi Kan's frontman Fork, for example, raps in one song, "Chemical material don't you shudder?/ Something awful is happening we don't suspect." In another, the group sings, "We can't control

MSG/ Our tongue has become paralyzed."[19] Rap is wildly popular in Japan, but Japanese youth are still trying to harness the kind of protest in their rap that characterizes rap in the United States.

Rap has even traveled back to its place of origin, Africa. American rap artists are extremely popular in Africa, and rap tapes and radio programs playing rap are the in thing among African youth. As in Europe, the rap of Africa incorporates the various influences of each country or region. In North Africa, the Moroccan rap group Aisha Kandisha blends the traditional music of that region, called *jajouka*, with the newer sounds of American rap. In South Africa, although the local rappers dress in the fashion of U.S. hip-hoppers, their music deals with the oppression and horrors of apartheid.

Rap has spread around the world, finding fans among the young people of every nation. It is the music of the young, the music of protest, and it is a music that can be produced cheaply with little formal knowledge of music. It is big business everywhere.

A few dollars more is what he started to make
Now he's drivin' around a Saab, with a house
    upstate
He got gold and diamond rings
Crazy girls and all those glamorous things
    — "A Few Dollars More," D Nice[1]

BY THE END OF THE TWENTIETH
century, many people felt that a great deal of rap
wasn't so much about the black experience anymore
as about money. As Evelyn McDonnell said, "It's
the new Hollywood, chinchilla stoles, diamonds
galore, stretch limos, Prada pumps: these are now
more than just the benefits of rap stardom, they're
the subject itself. . . . Gritty gangsta realism is
out; fabulous playa fantasy is in."[2] Open one of
the many magazines on rap—*Blaze, Vibe, The
Source*, or *Rap Pages*—and they are filled with
ads for clunky, glitzy, expensive jewelry, cars,
shoes, and upscale clothes—all the trappings of
high living. Although many critics, fans, and

musicians lament this show of extravagance and wealth, it is nothing new.

Since rap began, rappers have been cashing in on their success. Rap has been one of the few quick ways out of the city's poor black ghettos that does not involve crime or require some exceptional athletic or intellectual ability. If rappers cash in on their success, one can hardly blame them. In fact, they deserve a great deal of credit for their business acumen, knowledge of current recording technology, and their ability to take advantage of these. Rap marks the first time in the long history of black music in America that black musicians are getting some of what they deserve—and keeping it.

When the record industry began recording black musicians on "race" and rhythm and blues records, few black musicians were paid much money for their work, and most had no control over the means of production and distribution, the power within the recording industry. Unable to do their own recording, and at the mercy of the record companies, many lost control over the rights to their own music. Christopher John Farley, in his article "Hip-Hop Nation," an overview of contemporary rap in the late 1990s, facetiously writes, "[N]obody expects bluesmen to be moneymakers—that's why they're singing the blues."[3] Unfortunately, this flip attitude was also prevalent in the early days of the recording industry and continues to persist today. Artists aren't supposed to be rich, hence the widespread condemnation, usually by those with money already, of moneymaking rappers who flaunt their success and what Farley calls "rap's unabashed materialism."[4] The record industry hates to see that money slip through their fingers; the public wants its artists to suffer.

When rap music began, two things worked in its favor. First, established recording companies shunned the music. It was too "black," too much of a passing fad, they felt. It was not worth investing in. On the surface, this would seem to work against the music, but because the industry did not get involved, rappers and those interested in rap were forced to form their own recording companies, something the musicians of blues and jazz could not do because of their limited access to the recording technology.

A sound knowledge of recording technology was the other factor working in rap artists' favor. Because DJs worked constantly with sound and recording systems to actually create the music, they had a feel for and a knowledge of recording that earlier musicians lacked, and they had the necessary equipment or knew where to get it cheaply and easily. After being ignored by the established recording companies, startup labels such as Sugar Hill and Tommy Boy jumped into the gap, signing the new rap musicians, and the labels took off. One of the most successful was the brainchild of rapper-producer Sean "Puffy" or "Puff Daddy" Combs. His Bad Boy Records for a number of years was "one of hip-hop's most powerful new corporate dynasties."[5] Unfortunately, with the coming of the new millennium, Combs's enterprises began to falter in the wake of his own personal troubles. In the spring of 2000, Combs was indicted for carrying a concealed weapon and for the possession of an unlicensed weapon after an altercation outside a New York City nightclub.

Sean Combs was born in New York City. At the age of three, he lost his father, Melvin Combs, who was killed in a street deal gone bad. After the death of his father, Sean's mother, Janice Combs, moved him and his younger sister Keisha out of the city, into the suburbs. Janice Combs drove a school bus and sold clothes to support the family, and, with her mother, kept Sean off the streets and in school. Combs graduated from high school and attended Howard University, but admitted that he excelled only at throwing parties. In 1989, he dropped out of school and moved to New York, getting a job with Andre Harrell's Uptown Records, from which he launched Bad Boy Records in 1991. Combs, however, was ambitious and impatient, and in 1993, Harrell fired him. "He was hot tempered, very passionate," Harrell said, "very creative. But Puff was like Dennis the Menace. Every now and then something would get broken."[6] One thing that had "gotten broken" was an oversold party Combs had arranged with rapper Heavy D in 1991. The overcrowding resulted in a stampede in which nine people were killed. In 1999, a New York judge ruled that both Combs and Heavy D, as well as the sponsoring City College in New York, were responsible for the deaths. Although the judge levied no penalties or fines, the ruling opened the door to further civil law suits from the victims' families.

Combs licensed his Bad Boy Records to Arista Records and continued work on building his label. Three Bad Boy releases paved the way to success

Notorious B.I.G.

for Combs: Notorious B.I.G.'s *Life After Death*; Mase's *Harlem World*; and Combs's own *No Way Out*. Each record sold more than 3 million copies, and in 1997, "Combs's . . . elegy to B.I.G., who died in a drive-by shooting, outsold every other single that year except Elton John's tribute to Princess Diana."[7] The source of Combs's success was his intuitive sense of what would sell, of what listeners wanted, as well as his business acumen. Another ingredient of his success was his excitement over what he was doing. As he said in 1999, "There's never been an opportunity like this, even back in the Motown days. Very few people have the chance to be their own boss, to own what they create."[8]

That desire to own their own work, to control how it sounds, how it is marketed, is what has led many successful rappers to form their own production companies, once they have accumulated enough money. Frequently, once successful, these companies have been bought by the larger recording industry companies, with the original owners retaining artistic control of the labels. In the 1950s and '60s, records bore the labels of Columbia and RCA. Although many independent labels have been licensed to or taken over by larger conglomerates, rap's records today are marketed under a variety of new names: Rhino, Loud, Virgin, Def Jam, Priority, No Limit, Cash Money, Relativity, Tommy Boy, and of course, Bad Boy Records. Just as rap artists have taken over the means of production, they have also been able to seize a great deal of control over how their work is marketed, particularly in the field of music videos. Hip-hop has proved to be a boon to those black video and filmmakers who, before rap's popularity, were unable to get a foot in the door in video production.

The largest drawback to production of rap music has been in the use of sampling. The sampling used in the characteristic background music of rap has been a continual source of controversy. Some people have seen sampling as theft. Many rap groups have taken entire songs and simply placed raps over them. "Rapper's Delight" was set to the disco song "Good Times" by Chic. Chic sued the Sugarhill Gang for infringement of copyright and received $500,000 in compensation. After this, groups using older music were forced to pay royalties to its original composers, diminishing the amount a rap group and its recording company might earn. More recently, rap composers have begun creating their own original music. Before this, according to Rza of the group Wu-Tang Clan, sampling replenished "the old pots of gold for old artists. . . . [Now] we will be the songwriters of the future."[9]

Hip-hop and rap musicians have also profited in other areas from their notoriety. As more and more of young America has tuned into the music and the hip-hop scene, advertisers have taken notice. In 1994, "Sprite recast its ads to rely heavily on hip-hop themes. Its 1999 series of ads feature several up-and-coming rap stars (Common,

Fat Joe, Goodie Mob) in fast-moving animated clips that are intelligible only to viewers raised on Bone-Thugs-N-Harmony and Playstation."[10] Clothing advertisers, motorcycle makers, and a host of other manufacturers are cashing in on the culture, trying to make their products appear "phat" and cool enough to open the wallets of the youth of American, and various rappers and DJs are earning big bucks to promote them.

Hip-hop and rap are everywhere on the American landscape, in ads, film, on the television and radio, even on the internet. Thousands of Web sites have been created by record companies, fans, or by the artists themselves to advertise or discuss the music and the culture. Fans can visit the home pages of other fans and of rap artists from around the world, and hear some curious variations of rap music.

What has happened to rap, that musical alternative that shouted out the anger of the disenfranchised? It has become mainstream, become accepted. Today, despite his troubles, Sean "Puffy" Combs is rubbing elbows with Donald Trump, and Lauryn Hill is holding benefits for the nonprofit Refugee Project at Emporio Armani on New York's Fifth Avenue. Rapper Will Smith is one of the hottest actors in Hollywood, and Queen Latifah has her own talk show on television. All this success is the result of a great deal of hard work and is genuinely deserved, but does it spell the demise of rap, or show the continuing strength of its popularity?

```
Skiddlee beeboy a we rock a scoobie doo
And guess what, America, we love you
'Cause ya rocked and a rolled with so much soul
You could rock till you're a hundred and one
    years old
    — "Rapper's Delight," Sugarhill Gang[1]
```

rAP HAS BEEN CALLED THE MUSIC OF
the '90s, yet despite its proliferation, and its
musical and commercial success, there are those
who still feel that it is merely a passing fad and
will quickly disappear once the next fad appears.
But even if hip-hop's popularity fades, there will
always be those who wish to hear the originators of
rap, listen to the early raps, and study the many
variations of the genre—just as there will always
be lovers of the old country blues, ragtime, and
early jazz greats. Even without this core group, rap
is already transforming itself, evolving, as did every
other type of African American music in the past.

Rap is still going strong. Pick up any magazine specializing in rap, or even a general news

magazine, and you can find numerous articles showcasing new young talent and discussing the music. The appeal of the genre has not lessened, nor has the demand for the music—and new types of rap are constantly emerging. Some of the new subgenres of rap are strange indeed.

Considering the violence and anger of some of the early rap music, and of gangsta rap in particular, one of the oddest developments in rap is the evolution of Christian rap, a minor trend in the genre. In Christian rap, "hopeful musicians attach wholesome messages to potent beats."[2] Christian rappers have had some success, notably the trio DC Talk, a group from televangelist Jerry Falwell's Liberty University. They have recorded three albums, each of which has sold more than 500,000 copies. A number of Christian rap groups, and even one gangsta group, Gospel Gangstas, are made up of former L.A. gang members. In addition, "a bible using hip-hop vernacular,"[3] *Black Bible Chronicles: A Survival Manual for the Streets*, surfaced in 1993.

Despite such stylistic developments, the most important changes in rap now are in its technology, and it appears as though these changes will make the music more accessible to both artists and the public than ever before. When rap first began in

the 1970s, DJs developed the music behind the
rap by working with vinyl records on two turntables, scratching, backspinning, versioning, and
sampling. The 1970s, however, also saw the intro-
duction of the personal computer, and in its wake,
the rise of a wide variety of technology. By the late
1980s, DJs were creating mixes on digital turntables, and using computers to create even more
sounds. The young people born in the 1960s and
after took to this technology as if they had had the
instructions written in their very genes, despite
dire predictions by some critics. When rap began,
the records used were vinyl; with the digital revolution, rappers had to adapt to the new technology.
As rap scholar Harry Allen wrote,

> Hip-hop may be the first musical culture of the 20th cen-
> tury, or perhaps [in] history, to experience a material crisis due
> to a technology shift: from analog vinyl playback, which DJs
> use for cutting and scratching, to compact disc playback. It's
> almost certainly the first to experience such a crisis at the
> height of its popularity.[4]

The DJs and mixers of rap music took to the
new technology like ducks to water, despite the
ominous rumblings of those such as Allen. In
1999, however, a new element was added that
offered interesting possibilities both to established

rap artists and those hoping to break into the field, but caused consternation among the big record companies: MP3.

As Aliya S. King writes, the "MPEG 1 audio layer 3 . . . commonly known as MP3 [is] a format for encoding and compressing music files so they're small enough to store on portable players like the . . . Rio from Diamond Multimedia. The cell-phone-size player, which connects directly to your computer for downloading the music, offers CD-quality sound."[5] What this means is that fans can get their music directly from their computers rather than having to go to a music store. It is faster and much cheaper; the download cost of an album is estimated to be about $4.00, rather than say, the $15.95 price a store might charge.

However, the music industry views the MP3 with gloom. Steve Stoute of Interscope Records states, "It's something that could definitely damage the music industry. . . . The industry isn't ready [for MP3], the same way it wasn't ready for sampling. . . . They have to make rules and regulations to control the [new] technology, so that the artists and record companies get paid."[6] The problem is that, at present, *anyone* can post music on-line and *anyone* can download it. This has already resulted

in some pirated music. Thirteen new, unreleased
Nas songs in MP3 format were pirated and posted
on the internet more than two months before
Interscope Records released the new Nas album.[7]
Anyone could download them for free, much to
Interscope's distress. MP3 threatens the industry's
security, the livelihood of the distributor, as well as
the very existence of music stores.

The recording industry, of course, is not sitting
quietly:

> [T]he Big Five (BMG Entertainment, Sony Music, Warner
> Music Group, EMI Recorded Music, and Universal Music
> Group) formed the Secure Digital Music Initiative. This
> alliance (which controls 80 percent of the entire music indus-
> try) is scrambling to figure out how to commercially regulate
> digital distribution of music.[8]

More recently, a number of artists joined in to
fight this free distribution of their property. Rap
record producer Dr. Dre joined Metallica, together
with other artists and producers, in a suit against
Napster, which has been one of the most heavily
accessed Web sites for downloading free music.
He says, "As an artist there are so many ways that
we can be taken advantage of. To have yet one
more way to strip an artist of making an honest
living is just too much. That's why I sued."[9] The

recording industry and many of its artists are attempting to figure out a way to charge for the music being posted, and attempting to control or halt the distribution of pirated music.

Loud Records, however, sees MP3 as a boon to the industry. Randy Weiner, executive producer for new media for Loud, sees it as a way of making people aware of what is new. "It's all about getting people to hear the singles and buy the album," he has said, "and MP3 is a great way [to do that] without having radio stations tell us, 'Oh this doesn't fit our format.'"[10] Public Enemy, one of the earliest successful militant rap groups, agrees with this opinion. In November 1998, members of the group posted four tracks from their unreleased album, *Bring the Noise 2000*, on the Internet, offering them for free downloading. Def Jam, their recording company, objected strenuously and removed the tracks from the Internet, whereupon Public Enemy severed their twelve-year association with Def Jam. Chuck D of Public Enemy said, "The [industry is] running scared from the technology that evens out the creative field and makes artists harder to pimp."[11]

Besides ease of distribution, MP3 helps the

new, young artist just starting out who has no
record deal. All he or she has to do is post his or

her demo on-
line, then "get a
buzz, and then
offer your entire
album through
the MP3 format
for $3.00. Even
if only 20,000
people purchase
your album
(keep in mind,
the Internet
reaches mil-
lions), you're still
clearing $60,000
because you've
cut out all the
middlemen."[12]
In many ways,
MP3 has the
recording industry scared stiff.

Public
Enemy

    This kind of technological development will
only help rap music and the many young artists
who hope to break into the field and follow in the

footsteps of their idols. And since they already have a sure knowledge of today's (and often, tomorrow's) technology, they will have no problems adapting to it. In many ways, the technology is ideal for rap. Rap music started in the poorest sections of the cities in the United States. It began because young people had something to say and developed a music to go with their message, but they needed an outlet. Initially, the independent labels fulfilled that function. Now technology—MP3 and the Internet—can be their outlet. Rap artists can now be sure their voices will be carried around the world. As Chuck D has said, "The day of the demo is dead. You'll have a million artists and 500,000 labels on the Internet and everyone's gonna have to work harder to make it. . . . if you're not computer literate by the year 2000, you might as well be picking cotton."[13]

African American music has traveled a considerable distance, moving out from Africa and into every corner of the world; it was transmitted from the griots of early Africa to the griots of the modern world, the rappers, and it will most assuredly continue its journey. Rap is alive and well and just beginning to take advantage of the technological toys of today. As Chuck D has said,

As we head into the 21st century, rap music/hip-hop is in the earthwide sound stream, the child of soul, R and B, and rock 'n' roll, the by-product of the strategic marketing of Big Business, ready to pulse out to the millions on the wild, wild Web. It's difficult to stop a cultural revolution that bridges people together. Discussing differences through artistic communication and sharing interests in a common bond— rap music and hip-hop have achieved that in 20 years. . . . all you have to do is look around. Watch, feel and listen. It's only just begun.[14]

The genius of the music created by African Americans lies in its mutability, its ability to adapt and change to suit circumstances. Even today, rap is changing, with alternative rap supplanting earlier forms of rap, and young rappers creating their own music and labels utilizing the technology of the modern age. But whatever form rap takes tomorrow, it will, like earlier forms of black music, criticize and celebrate the world— and capture it with its appeal.

glossary

Alternative rap: Rap music of the 1990s and later that goes beyond sampling to incorporate other styles of music (jazz, rhythm and blues, rock).

Backspinning: Moving a record on the turntable so that important beats or phrases are repeated.

Battle: To compete in rapping, break dancing, and sometimes, in graffiti.

Battle rap: Verbally competitive rap music, often employing toasting, boasting, and rhyming snaps.

B-boys, B-girls: Shortened form of "break boy" or "break girl"; those who break dance; rap music fans or performers, male or female.

BG: Either "baby gangster" or "black gangster," depending upon the person being referred to.

Boasting: Bragging; using "boasts."

Boasts: Rhymes that brag about oneself and one's capabilities.

Boom box: A large, portable radio–tape player; also called a "ghetto blaster."

Break: Any part of a musical piece in which there is an instrumental solo, usually percussion.

Break dancing: An acrobatic, gymnastic style of dancing done to a heavy, percussive beat; from the "break" DJs often single out for the background music in rap.

Busta: A weak person, or someone who snitches on another.

Call and response: A technique, originating among the *griots* of West Africa, in which a solo verse line is alternated with a choral response, usually a short phrase or word.

Chill, chill out: Take it easy; cool it; relax.

Crew: Posse; a group of close friends or partners; the band and other members of a rap group.

Cut: A portion of a song that is played over and over again.

Def: Good or superior; cool.

Digital system: A combination of digital turntables and mixers used to create the background music in rap.

Dis: To disrespect someone; to criticize.

DJ: Disc jockey; the person who composes and/or controls the background music and sounds in a rap song.

Dope: Very cool.

Down: To agree with or be unified; to be involved with someone or something.

Dubbing: Cutting back and forth between the vocal and instrumental tracks of a record while adjusting the bass and treble for maximum effect.

Fly: Cool, hip, well-dressed, superior; from the 1970s film *Superfly*.

Flygirl: A female rapper; a hip, cool woman.

Freestyle rap: Improvisational rap, often done as a response to a challenge issued by another rapper.

Fresh: Cool, outstanding, stylish.

Frontin': Putting up a front, a mask; being deceptive.

G: Close friend, girlfriend.

Gangsta rap: A style of rap originating in South Central Los Angeles. It is characterized by the use of obscenities and by expressions and depictions of violence. Most gangsta raps deal with life in the 'hood and all that goes with it: sex, drugs, alcohol, guns, and gang violence.

Ganja: White; white establishment; marijuana.

***Griot* (masc.), *Griotte* (fem.):** Male and female professional singers and storytellers of West Africa.

Hip-hop: Rap music; a way of life that includes break dancing and rapping.

'Ho: Whore, prostitute.

Homeboy, homey: A friend from your neighborhood, someone you grew up with.

'Hood: Neighborhood.

In the house: In the club, dance place, neighborhood; a phrase used to acknowledge the presence of one's peers, or a special guest.

Jam, jamming: A song; singing, making music.

Juice: Power.

Kicks: Shoes.

MC: A rap performer, from "master of ceremonies," as on television. Sometimes spelled "emcee."

Message rap: Rap music that tries to communicate with and warn its audience about social and political ills.

Old school rap: The style of rap characteristic of rap's early days. It is more positive, less political, and less angry than later rap music.

Phat: Cool; the latest, most up-to-date.

Playa rap: Rap that is concerned with money and materialism.

Play the dozens: To jokingly taunt someone by kidding, "jiving," teasing, or insulting his or her family; to use "snaps." (See *Snapping*.)

Posse: See *Crew*.

Punch phrasing: Taking a certain part of a recording that features a vocal, horn, or drum solo and repeating it regularly throughout a particular piece of music.

Punk rap: A combination of heavy metal, synthesizer rock, and rap.

Ragga: A fast-tempoed style of British rap with a heavy bass that combines a Caribbean flavor with an aggressive black awareness.

Rap: A combination of rhymed lyrics over rhythm tracks and pieces of recorded music and sounds called samples.

Raptivist: Term coined by Sister Souljah, meaning a rap activist.

Reggae: Music of Jamaican origin that combines native styles with rock and soul.

Sampling: Taking bits and pieces of previously recorded music and inserting them into the background of a song, sometimes over and over again.

Scratching: Manually moving a record back and forth under the needle to produce a scratching beat.

Signifying: Insulting another person, sometimes in rhyme, using snaps that are insulting to that person.

Snap(s): Insulting someone jokingly. (See *Snapping*.)

Snapping: Insulting someone jokingly, usually by referring insultingly to that person's relatives, especially their mother. (See also *Play the dozens*.)

Sound systems: A group consisting of an MC, DJ, roadies, engineers, and bouncers who played records and toasted at dances and clubs in Jamaica.

Toasts: Humorous rhyming stories, sometimes lengthy, told mostly among men and used to entertain, but also, at times, to insult and taunt.

Trip-hop: A British rap style; a slow dance rap expressing social and romantic anger.

Versioning: A type of sampling in which old and new music is mixed together. Unlike sampling, however, versioning usually involves reworking an entire composition.

Wack: Stupid, uncool, bogus, or poorly done.

Word, word up: An expression signifying agreement, understanding.

Endnotes

1. Boo-yaa Tribe. "New Funky Nation," in *Rap: The Lyrics*, Lawrence A. Stanley, ed. New York: Penguin Books, 1992: 46.

1. rockin' it

1. Fearless Four. "Rockin' It," in Stanley, *op. cit.*:129.

2. Stanley: xxxix.

3. "Rap Music." *The New Grolier Multimedia Encyclopedia*. CD-ROM. Novato, Ca.: Software Toolworks/Grolier Electronic Publishing, Inc.: 1993.

4. Rose, Tricia. *Black Noise: Rap Music and Black Culture in Contemporary America*. Hanover, N.H.: University Press of New England/Wesleyan University Press, 1994: 2.

5. Kane, Big Daddy. "Smooth Operator," in Stanley: 21.

6. Rose: 65.

7. *Ibid.*: 66.

8. *Ibid.*: 88.

9. Heavy D and the Boyz. "We Got Our Own Thang," in Stanley: 157.

10. James, Jimmy. *The History of Rap.* http://www.geocities.com/SunsetStrip/Palladium/8153/raphistory.htm. Accessed 20 January 1999.

11. Farley, Christopher John. "Hip-Hop Nation," *Time*, 8 February 1999: 56.

12. *Ibid.*: 57.

2. african rhythms

1. Sister Souljah, "Sister Souljah,"
http://www.altculture.com/.index/aentries/s/sisterxsou.html.
Accessed 24 February 1999.

2. "About *Griots*: Paul Oliver." *Savannah Syncopators.*
http://www.wlu.edu/~hblackme/griot/oliver.html.
Accessed 28 January 1999.

3. Bender, Wolfgang. *Sweet Mothers*. Chicago: University
of Chicago Press, 1991: 17–18.

4. Jones, K. Maurice. *Say It Loud!* Brookfield, Conn.: The
Millbrook Press, 1994: 19.

5. Eastman, Ralph. *African Influences in the Development
of American Music as Illustrated in Early Delta Blues
Performances.*
http://olympia.9se.uci.edu/lessons/blues.html.
Accessed 10 January 1999.

6. Jones: 24.

7. Lomax, Alan. *The Folk Songs of North America in the
English Language.* Garden City, N.Y.: Doubleday & Co., 1960:
470.

8. Jones: 22–23.

9. Eastman.

10. *The American Heritage Songbook*. New York:
American Heritage Publishing Co., 1969: 79.

11. Berlin, Edward A. "Ragtime," in *New Grolier
Multimedia Encyclopedia.*

12. *The American Heritage Songbook*: 142.

13. Lomax: 573, 574.

14. Jones: 29.

15. Ivey, Donald J. "Blues," in *New Grolier Multimedia Encyclopedia.*

16. Lomax: 575.

17. Eastman.

18. Ivey, Donald J. "Jazz," *New Grolier Multimedia Encyclopedia.*

19. *Ibid.*

20. Rose, Tricia, *op. cit.*: 133.

21. Farley, Christopher John, with Ginia Bellafante. "Hip-Hop Goes Bebop," *Time*, 12 July 1993. Time Almanac, Reference Edition. CD-ROM. Fort Lauderdale, Fla.: Compact Publishing / Time Magazine, 1994.

22. Ivey.

23. Eastman.

24. Toop, David E. *The Rap Attack: African Jive to New York Hip-hop.* Boston: South End Press, 1984: 38.

25. Berlin, Edward A. "Rock Music," in *New Grolier Multimedia Encyclopedia.*

3. soul to hip-hop

1. Sub Sonic 2. "Unsung Heroes of Hip-hop," in Stanley: *op. cit.*: 317.

2. Toop, *op. cit.*: 84.

3. Baulch, Vivian M. "The Golden Age of the Motown Sound," *Rearview Mirror*. Detroit, Mich.: *The Detroit News*. http://www.detnews.com/history/motown/motown.htm. Accessed 24 March 1999.

4. "Soul Music," in *New Grolier Multimedia Encyclopedia.*

5. Baulch.

6. Jones, *op. cit.*: 38.

7. *Ibid.*

8. *Ibid.*: 45.

9. Rhodes, Henry A. "The Evolution of Rap Music in the United States." *Yale–New Haven Teachers Institute*, 1998. http://www.cis.yale.edu/ynhti/curriculum/units/1993/4/94.04.04 .html#a. Accessed 24 March 1999.

10. Larkin, Colin. *The Virgin Encyclopedia of Reggae.* London: Virgin Books, 1998: 245.

11. Habekost, Christian "Chako." "Rapso, Riddim Poetry from Trinidad/Tobago," *The Beat*, vol. 12, no. 2, 1993: 42–44.

12. Rhodes.

13. *Ibid.*

14. *Ibid.*

15. *Ibid.*

16. Fresh, Mr., & The Supreme Rockers. *Breakdancing.* New York: Avon, 1984.

17. *Ibid.*

4. toasts, boasts, and snaps

1. Sugarhill Gang. "Rapper's Delight," in Stanley, *op. cit.*: 325.

2. Toop, *op. cit.*: 29.

3. "Some History About Playing the Dozens," *Online Magazine*, Accessed 12 December 1998.

4. Quoted in Toop: 32.

5. Rhodes, *op. cit.*

6. *Ibid.*

7. *Ibid.*

8. Quoted in Rhodes.

9. *On a Mission: Selected Poems and a History of The Last Poets.* http://www.fsbassociates.com/books/poets.htm. Accessed 20 December 1998.

10. Jones, *op. cit.*: 35.

11. Quoted in Jones: 36–37.

5. raps and rappers

1. Fresh, Doug E. "The Greatest Entertainer," in Stanley, *op. cit.*: 98.

2. Stanley: xxi.

3. Quoted in Toop, *op. cit.*: 63, 65.

4. Stanley: xxii.

5. Quoted in Greenberg, Keith Elliot. *Rap.* Minneapolis: Lerner Publications Co., 1988: 25.

6. "Noize Makers of 1998." *Rap Pages,* January 1999: 22–75.

7. Quoted in Jones, *op. cit.*: 58.

8. *Ibid:* 65.

9. "Noize Makers of 1998": 22–75.

10. Croal, N'Gai. "Method to the Madness." *Newsweek,* 16 November 1998: 79.

11. Sixth Sense Creations. *Styles.* 1996. http://osiris.colorado.edu/~beerball/rap/styles.html. Accessed 11 December 1998.

12. Farley, Christopher John, with Ginia Bellafante, *op. cit.*

13. Croal: 86.

14. "The Best of Music." *Time,* 21 December 1998: 84.

15. "Hip-Hop Hope." *New York,* 21 December 1998: 95.

16. "Noize Makers of 1998": 23.

17. Samuels, Allison. "Taking Rap Back to Its Real Roots." *Newsweek,* 15 March 1999: 68.

6. queendoms of rap

1. Queen Latifah. "Come Into My House," in Stanley, *op. cit.*: 265.

2. Toop, *op. cit.*: 121.

3. Stanley: xxvii.

4. Jones, *op. cit.*: 68.

5. Stanley: 286.

6. Quoted in Greenberg, *op. cit.*: 30.

7. *Ibid.*

8. Jones: 70.

9. Stanley: 267.

10. Quoted in White, Jack E. "Sister Souljah: Capitalist Tool." *Time.* 29 June 1992. *Time Almanac Reference Edition.*

11. *Ibid.*

12. "Sister Souljah."
http://www.altculture.com/.index/aentries/s/sisterxsou.html.
Accessed 24 February 1999.

13. McDonnell, Evelyn. "Fox on the Run." *The Village Voice,* 9 February 1999: 115.

14. *Ibid.*

15. "Lil' Kim: Rap's Pocket Rocket." *The Sunday Monitor: Monitor—A Young People's Supplement.* 18 January 1998.
http://www.africanews.com/monitor/freeissues/19jan98/
monitor.html.
Accessed 5 March 1999.

16. "Missy Elliott."
http://www.altculture.com/.index/aentries/m/missy.html.
Accessed 10 March 1999.

17. "Noize Makers of 1998." *Rap Pages*. January 1999: 42.

18. Farley, Christopher John. "Lauryn Hill." *Time*,
8 February 1998: 59.

19. Quoted in Farley, *ibid.*

7. rappin' 'round the world

1. Vanilla Ice. "Ice, Ice Baby," in Stanley, *op. cit.*: 381.

2. Jones, *op. cit.*: 73.

3. Toop, *op. cit.*: 137.

4. Thigpen, David E. "Raps, in Blue." *Newsweek*, 5 April
1999: 70.

5. *Ibid.*

6. Farley, Christopher John. "A Whiter Shade of Pale."
Time, 29 May 2000: 73.

7. "Speaking With the Devil." *Newsweek*, 5 June 2000: 70.

8. Cocks, Jay, with Ian McCluskey, and Stacy Perman.
"Rap Around the Globe." *Time*, 19 October 1992. *Time
Almanac Reference Edition.*

9. Beau, Marie-Agnés. "Hip-hop Rap in Europe."
Euromusic: E.M.O.
http://www.euromusic.com /EMO/mcseurope/eight.htm.
Accessed 28 February 1999.

10. "Bristol Trip-Hop."
http://www.altculture.com/aentries/b/bristol.html.
Accessed 3 March 1999.

11."Roots of Trip-Hop." *Salon Magazine,*
12 November 1995.
http://www.salonmagazine.com12nov1995/reviews/triphop2.html.
Accessed 3 March 1999.

12. Cocks.

13. *Ibid.*

14. Beau, *op. cit.*

15. *Ibid.*

16. Quoted in Dookey, Spence. *Solaar Energy: Words with
MC Solaar.* http://www.jetpack.com/02/ beats/solaar/.
Accessed 3 March 1999.

17. Cocks.

18. *Ibid.*

19. *Ibid.*

8. glamorous things

1. D Nice. "A Few Dollars More," in Stanley, *op. cit.*: 62.

2. McDonnell, Evelyn. "Fox on the Run." *The Village
Voice,* 9 February 1999: 115.

3. Farley, Christopher John. "Hip-Hop Nation." *Time,*
8 February 1999: 57.

4. *Ibid.*

5. Thigpen, David E. "Puffy." *Newsweek,* 8 February
1999: 63.

6. *Ibid.*

7. *Ibid.*

8. Quoted in
Thigpen, *ibid.*

9. Quoted in Roberts,

Johnnie L. "The Rap on Rap." *Newsweek,* 1 March 1999: 45.

10. Farley: 58.

9. rappin' on

1. Sugarhill Gang. "Rapper's Delight." in Stanley, *op. cit.*: 320.

2. "Christian Rap." http://www.altculture.com/index/aentries/c/christxra.html. Accessed 5 February 1999.

3. *Ibid.*

4. Quoted in Freund, Jesse. "Chip-hop." *Wired.* September 1997. http://www.wired.com/wired/ 5.09/chiphop.html. Accessed 20 December 1998.

5. King, Aliya S. "MP3 and Hip-Hop: Sounds Like the Future." *The Source,* 115, April 1999: 45.

6. Quoted in Babcock, Jay. "My MP3 Weighs a Ton." *Vibe,* May 1999: 49.

7. *Ibid.*

8. King, *op. cit.*

9. Quoted in Levy, Steven. "The Noisy War Over Napster." *Newsweek,* 5 June 2000: 51.

10. Quoted in Babcock.

11. *Ibid.*

12. Quoted in King.

13. King.

14. Chuck D, Public Enemy. "The Sound of Our Young World." *Newsweek,* 8 February 1999: 66.

"About *Griots*: Paul Oliver." *Savannah Syncopators*.
   http://www.wlu.edu/~hblackme/griot/oliver.html.
   Accessed 28 January 1999.

The American Heritage Songbook. New York: American
   Heritage Publishing Co., 1969

Babcock, Jay. "My MP3 Weighs a Ton." *Vibe*,
   May, 1999: 49.

Baulch, Vivian M. "The Golden Age of the Motown Sound."
   Rearview Mirror. *The Detroit News*.
   http://www.detnews.com/history/motown/motown.htm.
   Accessed 24 March 1999.

Beau, Marie-Agnés. "Hip-hop Rap in Europe."
   Euromusic: E.M.O.
   http://www.euromusic.com/EMO/mcseurope/eight.htm.
   Accessed 28 February 1999.

Bender, Wolfgang. *Sweet Mothers*. Chicago: University of
   Chicago Press, 1991.

Berlin, Edward A. "Ragtime." *New Grolier Multimedia
   Encyclopedia*. CD-ROM. Novato, Calif.: The Software
   Toolworks, Inc. / Grolier, Inc., 1993.

———. "Rock Music." *New Grolier Multimedia Encyclopedia*.
   CD-ROM. Novato, Calif.: The Software Toolworks, Inc. /
   Grolier, Inc., 1993.

"The Best of Music." *Time*, 21 December 1998: 54.

"Bristol/Trip-Hop."
http://www.altculture.com/aentries/b/bristol.html.
Accessed 3 March 1999.

"Brown, James." *New Grolier Multimedia Encyclopedia.* CD-ROM. Novato, Calif.: The Software Toolworks, Inc. / Grolier, Inc., 1993.

"Can Battle Rap Be a Part of Christianity?" *Street Wizdom's Urban Jungle.* gw@streetwizdom.com.
Accessed 10 December 1998.

Caviness, Oyama. *There Ain't Nothin' Like Hip-hop Music.*
http://www.engl.virginia.edu/~enwr1016/osc2x/hiphop.html.
Accessed 11 January 1999.

"Christian Rap."
http://www.altculture.com/.index/aentries/c/christxra.html.
Accessed 5 February 1999.

Chuck D., Public Enemy. "The Sound of Our Young World."
Newsweek, 8 February 1999: 66.

Cocks, Jay, with Ian McCluskey, & Stacy Perman. "Rap Around the Globe." *Time*, 19 October 1992. *Time Almanac Reference Edition.* CD-ROM. Washington, D.C.: Compact Publishing / Time Magazine Co., Inc., 1994.

Cooper, Carol. "Do for Self." *The Village Voice*, October 1–13, 1998.
http://www.villagevoice.com/arts/ 9841/cooper.shtml.
Accessed 11 January 1999.

Croal, N'Gai. "Method to the Madness." *Newsweek*, 16
    November 1998: 86.

"Disco Music." *New Grolier Multimedia Encyclopedia*. CD-
    ROM. Novato, Calif.: The Software Toolworks, Inc. /
    Grolier, Inc., 1993.

Dookey, Spence. *Solaar Energy: Words with MC Solaar*.
    http://www.jetpack.com/02/beats/solaar/.
    Accessed 3 March 1999.

Eastman, Ralph. *African Influences in the Development of
    American Music as Illustrated in Early Delta Blues
    Performances*.
    http://olympia.9se.uci.edu/Lessons/blues.html.
    Accessed 10 January 1999.

Farley, Christopher John. "A Whiter Shade of Pale." *Time*, 29
    May 2000: 73.

————, with Ginia Bellafante. "Hip-Hop Goes Bebop." *Time*,
    12 July 1993. *Time Almanac, Reference Edition*. CD-ROM.
    Fort Lauderdale, Fla.: Compact Publishing/Time Magazine,
    1994.

————. "Hip-Hop Nation." *Time*, 8 February 1999: 54–64.

————. "Lauryn Hill." *Time*, 8 February 1998: 58–59.

Freund, Jesse. "Chip-hop." *Wired*. September 1997.
    http://www.wired.com/wired/5.09/chiphop.html.
    Accessed 20 December 1998.

"Gangsta."
http://www.altculture.com/.index/aentries/g/gangsta.html.
Accessed 6 March 1999.

Greenberg, Keith Elliot. *Rap*. Minneapolis: Lerner Publications
Co., 1988.

Habekost, Christian "Chako." "Rapso, Riddim Poetry from
Trinidad/Tobago." *The Beat*, 12, 2, 1993: 42–44.

Haring, Bruce. "Is the Rivalry Escalating Despite So-called
Truce?" *USA Today*, 10 March 1997.
www.hip-hop.com/section302/archive_articles/
rapperworriesaboutdeath.html.
Accessed 4 January 1999.

"Hip-Hop Hope." *New York*, 21 December 1998: 95.

Holloway, Carolyn. *Dropping Knowledge in the '90s: Chuck D
Lectures at N.C. State*.
http://www.sma.ncstate.net/Nubian/A...ng1998/021998/
Headlines/chuckd.html.
Accessed 24 November 1998.

Ivey, Donald J. "Blues." *New Grolier Multimedia
Encyclopedia*. CD-ROM. Novato,: The Software Toolworks,
Inc. / Grolier, Inc., 1993.

"Jazz." *New Grolier Multimedia Encyclopedia*. CD-ROM. Novato,
Calif.: The Software Toolworks, Inc. / Grolier, Inc., 1993.

James, Jimmy. *The History of Rap*.
http://www.geocities.com/SunsetStrip/Palladium/8153/
raphistory.htm.
Accessed 20 January 1999.

Jones, Maurice, K. *Say It Loud!* Brookfield, Conn.:
The Millbrook Press, 1994.

Kamin, Jonathan. "Reggae." *New Grolier Multimedia
Encyclopedia.* CD-ROM. Novato, Calif.: The Software
Toolworks, Inc. / Grolier, Inc., 1993.

————. "Rhythm and Blues." *New Grolier Multimedia
Encyclopedia.* CD-ROM. Novato, Calif.: The Software
Toolworks, Inc. / Grolier, Inc., 1993.

King, Aliya S. King. "MP3 and Hip-Hop: Sounds Like the
Future." *The Source,* 115, April 1999: 45.

Levy, Steven. "The Nosy War Over Napster." *Newsweek,*
5 June 2000: 46–53.

"Lil Kim: Rap's Pocket Rocket." *The Sunday Monitor:
Monitor—A Young People's Supplement.* 18 January 1998.
http://www.africanews.com/monitor/freeissues/18jan98/
monitor.html.
Accessed 5 March 1999.

Lomax, Alan. *The Folk Songs of North America in the English
Language.* Garden City, N.Y.: Doubleday & Co., 1960.

Mann, Jeff "The Man." *It Ain't True, Like Kung Fu: The
Underground Rap Scene Explained.*
http://www. santacruzhs.santacruz.k12.ca.us/trident/
2-95/kungfu.html.
Accessed 24 November 1998.

McDonnell, Evelyn. "Fox on the Run." *The Village Voice,* 9
February 1999: 115.

"Missy Elliott."

> http://www.altculture.com/.index/aentries/m/missy.html.
> Accessed 10 March 1999.

Mr. Fresh and the Supreme Rockers. *Breakdancing.* New
> York: Avon Books, 1984.

"New Directions for The Next Decade." *Time,* 4 September
> 1989. *Time Almanac Reference Edition.* CD-ROM.
> Washington, D.C.: Compact Publishing / Time Magazine Co.,
> Inc., 1994.

Noel, Peter. "Revenge of the Mad Rappers." *The Village Voice,*
> November 24–30, 1998.
> http://www.villagevoice.com/feature/9848/noel.shtml.
> Accessed 11 January 1999.

"Noize Makers of 1998." *Rap Pages,* January 1999: 22–75.

On a Mission: Selected Poems and a History of The Last Poets.
> http://www.fsbassociates.com/books/poets.htm.
> Accessed 20 December 1998.

Peyser, Marc, with Alisha Davis and Allison Samuels.
> "Newsmakers: Another Parks Protest." *Newsweek,* 12 April
> 1999: 57.

"Queen Latifah."
> http://www.altculture.com/aentries/q/queenxlati.html.
> Accessed 10 March 1999.

"Rap Music." *RAP Music: Basic Information and Quotations.*
> http://www.learn-line.nrw.de/Faecher/English/
> Rap/basicinf.htm.
> Accessed 17 November 1998.

"Rap Music." *Rap Music for MusicSource.*
    http://tqd.advanced.org/3387/rap_nf.html.
    Accessed 20 December 1998.

"Rap Music." *New Grolier Multimedia Encyclopedia.*
    CD-ROM. Novato, Calif.: Software Toolworks, Inc. /
    Grolier Electronic Publishing, Inc., 1993.

Rhodes, Henry A. "The Evolution of Rap Music in the United
    States." Yale–New Haven Teachers Institute, 1998.
    http://www.cis.yale.edu/ynhti/curriculum/units/1993/4/
    93.04.04.x.html#a.
    Accessed 24 March 1999.

Roberts, Johnnie L. "The Rap on Rap." *Newsweek*, 1 March
    1999: 44-45.

"The Roots of Trip-Hop." *Salon Magazine*, 12 November
    1995. http://www.salonmagazine.com/12nov 1995/
    reviews/triphop2.html. Accessed 3 March 1999.

Rose, Tricia. *Black Noise: Rap Music and Black Culture in
    Contemporary America.* Hanover, N.H.: University Press
    of New England/Wesleyan University Press, 1994.

"The Salt-n-Pepa Story." *Salt-N-Pepa's Homepage.*
    http://www.execpc.com/~mwildt/bio.html.
    Accessed 28 February 1999.

Samuels, Allison. "Taking Rap Back to Its Real Roots."
    Newsweek, 15 March 1999: 68.

Saunders, Jeff K. *The Rap Music War.*
    http://Ez.starhosting.com/mm/rapmusic.html.
    Accessed 10 January 1999.

"Sister Souljah."
http://www.altculture.com/.index/aentries/s/sisterxsou.html.
Accessed 24 February 1999.

Sixth Sense Creations. *Styles*. 1996.
http://osiris.colorado.edu/~beerball/rap/styles.html.
Accessed 11 December 1998.

Small, Nadell, Bonnie Small and John Small. *Breakdance: Do It!*
Philadelphia: A Quarto Book, 1984.

"Some History About Playing the Dozens." *Online Magazine.*

"Soul Music." *The New Grolier Multimedia Encyclopedia.*
CD-ROM. Novato, Calif.: The Software Toolworks, Inc. /
Grolier, Inc., 1993.

"Speaking With the Devil." *Newsweek*, 5 June 2000: 70.

Stanley, Lawrence A., ed. *Rap: The Lyrics*. New York: Penguin
Books, 1992.

The Totally Unofficial Rap Dictionary.
http://www.sci.kin.nl/thalia/rapdict/dictionary_m.html.
Accessed 20 December 1998.

Thigpen, David E. "Raps, in Blue." *Newsweek*, 5 April
1999: 70.

———. "Puffy." *Newsweek*, 8 February 1999: 63.

Toop, David. *The Rap Attack: African Jive to New York Hip-hop.*
Boston: South End Press, 1984.

"A Working Hip-Hop Chronology." *Professa Rap's Working Hip-Hop Chronology.* http://www.ai.mit.edu/~isbell/HFh/hiphop/rap_history.html. Accessed 12 February 1999.

White, Jack E. "Sister Souljah: Capitalist Tool." *Time,* 29 June 1992. Time Almanac Reference Edition. CD-ROM. Washington, D.C.: Compact Publishing / Time Magazine Co., Inc., 1994.

photo credits

page 5   Big Daddy Kane: MICHAEL OCHS ARCHIVES/
            Venice, Calif.

page 14   "Manner of Playing the Ka" from Lafcadio Hearn,
            Two Years in the French West Indies (1890).
            Reproduced by permission of *The Huntington
            Library*, San Marino, Calif.

page 21   "A Negro Festival drawn from Nature in the Island
            of St. Vincent" from Bryan Edwards, *The History . . .
            of the British West Indies*. 1801. Reproduced by
            permission of *The Huntington Library*, San Marino,
            Calif.

page 29   Louis Armstrong: from James Lincoln Collier, *Louis
            Armstrong: An American Genius* (Oxford University
            Press: New York, 1983)

page 32   Charlie Parker: courtesy of the James Haskins
            Collection.

page 39   James Brown and the Famous Flames: courtesy of
            the Frank Driggs Collection.

page 48   Break dancer: AP/Wide World Photos.

page 58   IRT 3 train: Marguerite Lavin.

page 68   The Sugarhill Gang: MICHAEL OCHS ARCHIVES/
            Venice, Calif.

index

Page numbers in italic type refer to pages with illustrations